1. Mugger crocodile (*Crocodylus palustris*)

2. Saltwater crocodile (*Crocodylus porosus*)

3. Gharial (*Gavialis gangeticus*)

4. Three-striped roofed turtle (*Kachuga dhongoka*)

5. Indian roofed turtle (*Kachuga tecta*)

6. River terrapin (*Batagur baska*)

7. Indian star tortoise (*Geochelone elegans*)

8. Sri Lankan bent-toed gecko (*Cyrtodactylus frenatus*)

9. Andamans bent-toed gecko (*Cyrtodactylus rubidus*)

10. Termite hill gecko (*Hemidactylus triedrus*)

11. Green forest lizard (*Calotes calotes*)

12. Painted forest lizard (*Calotes ceylonensis*)

13. Whistling forest lizard (*Calotes liolepis*)

14. Stoddart's horned lizard (*Ceratophora stoddartii*)

15. Sri Lankan dwarf lizard (*Cophotis ceylanica*)

16. Fan-throated lizard (*Sitana ponticeriana*)

17. Indian spiny-tailed lizard (*Uromastyx hardwickii*)

18. Indian chamaeleon (*Chamaeleo zeylanicus*)

19. Knuckles limbless skink (*Chalcidoseps thwaitesii*)

20. Deceptive Sri Lankan skink (*Lankascincus fallax*)

21. Andamans giant skink (*Mabuya tytleri*)

26. Indian rock python (*Python molurus*)

27. Olive keelback water snake (*Atretium schistosum*)

28. Forstein's cat snake
(*Boiga forsteni*)

29. Ornate flying snake
(*Chrysopelea ornata*)

30. Blue bronzeback tree snake
(*Dendrelaphis cyanochloris*)

31. Common bronzeback tree snake (*Dendrelaphis tristis*) [eating a bark gecko (*Hemidactylus leschenaulti*)]

32. Half-lined kukri snake (*Oligodon sublineatus*)

33. Spectacled cobra (*Naja naja*)

34. Yellow-lipped sea krait (*Laticauda colubrina*)

35. Hump-nosed pit viper (*Hypnale hypnale*)

36. Sri Lankan green pit viper (*Trimeresurus trigonocephala*)

BIOGEOGRAPHY OF THE REPTILES OF SOUTH ASIA

by
Indraneil Das
Department of Organismic and Evolutionary Biology
Museum of Comparative Zoology
Harvard University

KRIEGER PUBLISHING COMPANY
MALABAR, FLORIDA
1996

Cover: Montane trinket snake (*Elaphe helena monticollaris*). Photo: Indraneil Das

Original Edition 1996

Printed and Published by
**KRIEGER PUBLISHING COMPANY
KRIEGER DRIVE
MALABAR, FLORIDA 32950**

Copyright © 1996 by Krieger Publishing Company

All rights reserved. No part of this book may be reproduced in any form or by any means, electronic or mechanical, including information storage and retrieval systems without permission in writing from the publisher.
No liability is assumed with respect to the use of the information contained herein.
Printed in the United States of America.

FROM A DECLARATION OF PRINCIPLES JOINTLY ADOPTED BY A COMMITTEE OF THE AMERICAN BAR ASSOCIATION AND COMMITTEE OF PUBLISHERS:

This Publication is designed to provide accurate and authoritative information in regard to the subject matter covered. It is sold with the understanding that the publisher is not engaged in rendering legal, accounting, or other professional service. If legal advice or other expert assistance is required, the services of a competent professional person should be sought.

Library of Congress Cataloging-in-Publication Data
Das, Indraneil, 1964–
   Biogeography of the reptiles of South Asia / by Indraneil Das.
       p. cm.
   Includes bibliographical references and index.
   ISBN 0-89464-935-3 (alk. paper)
   1. Reptiles—South Asia—Geographical distribution. I. Title.
QL661.S64D37 1996
597.9'0954—dc20
                                                94-48209
                                                   CIP

10 9 8 7 6 5 4 3 2

CONTENTS

List of Plates	iv
The Author	vi
Acknowledgments	vii
1. Introduction	1
2. Methods	3
3. Physiographic Zones	5
4. Results and Discussion	15
4.1. Biodiversity and Endemicity	15
4.2. Faunal Characteristics of Physiographic Zones	20
4.3. Patterns and Correlates of Diversity	24
4.4. Affinities between Physiographic Zones	25
4.5. Affinities with Extralimital Fauna	28
4.6. Barriers and Speciation	31
4.7. Disjunct Distribution of Taxa	34
5. Tables	37
Table 1. Checklist of Reptiles of South Asia	37
Table 2. Taxonomic Composition and Endemicity of the Reptiles of South Asia	64
Table 3. Species Richness of Reptiles of South Asia and Their Focus	65
Table 4. Endemic Genera and Number of Endemic Reptile Species in South Asia	66
Table 5. Affinities of the Non-endemic Reptile Genera in South Asia	68
Table 6. Representation of Extralimital Reptile Genera in the Four Northern Zones of South Asia	72
Table 7. Species Pairs of Reptiles from South Asia and Adjacent Regions Showing Sister Species Boundaries and Presumed Mode of Speciation	73
6. Summary	75
References	77
Index	87

PLATES

1. Mugger crocodile (*Crocodylus palustris*)
2. Saltwater crocodile (*Crocodylus porosus*)
3. Gharial (*Gavialis gangeticus*)
4. Three-striped roofed turtle (*Kachuga dhongoka*)
5. Indian roofed turtle (*Kachuga tecta*)
6. River terrapin (*Batagur baska*)
7. Indian star tortoise (*Geochelone elegans*)
8. Sri Lankan bent-toed gecko (*Cyrtodactylus frenatus*)
9. Adamans bent-toed gecko (*Cyrtodactylus rubidus*)
10. Termite hill gecko (*Hemidactylus triedrus*)
11. Green forest lizard (*Calotes calotes*)
12. Painted forest lizard (*Calotes ceylonensis*)
13. Whistling forest lizard (*Calotes liolepis*)
14. Stoddart's horned lizard (*Ceratophora stoddartii*)
15. Sri Lankan dwarf lizard (*Cophotis ceylanica*)
16. Fan-throated lizard (*Sitana ponticeriana*)
17. Indian spiny-tailed lizard (*Uromastyx hardwickii*)
18. Indian chamaeleon (*Chamaeleo zeylanicus*)
19. Knuckles limbless skink (*Chalcidoseps thwaitesii*)
20. Deceptive Sri Lankan skink (*Lankascincus fallax*)
21. Andamans giant skink (*Mabuya tytleri*)
22. Land monitor (*Varanus bengalensis*) [eating an Asian house gecko (*Hemidactylus frenatus*)]
23. Sri Lankan pipe snake (*Cylindrophis maculata*)
24. Drummond-Hay's shieldtail (*Rhinophis drummondhayi*)
25. Whitaker's sand boa (*Eryx whitakeri*)
26. Indian rock python (*Python molurus*)
27. Olive keelback water snake (*Atretium schistosum*)

28. Forstein's cat snake (*Boiga forsteni*)
29. Ornate flying snake (*Chrysopelea ornata*)
30. Blue bronzeback tree snake (*Dendrelaphis cyanochloris*)
31. Common bronzeback tree snake (*Dendrelaphis tristis*) [eating a bark gecko (*Hemidactylus leschenaulti*)]
32. Half-lined kukri snake (*Oligodon sublineatus*)
33. Spectacled cobra (*Naja naja*)
34. Yellow-lipped sea krait (*Laticauda colubrina*)
35. Hump-nosed pit viper (*Hypnale hypnale*)
36. Sri Lankan green pit viper (*Trimeresurus trigonocephala*)

All photographs: Indraneil Das

THE AUTHOR

Indraneil Das received his doctorate in zoology from the University of Oxford for his work on community ecology. Between December 1991 and September 1993, he was with Universiti Brunei Darussalam, conducting a study of the distribution and ecology of rainforest amphibians and reptiles of Borneo. Currently, Dr. Das is a Fulbright Fellow at Harvard University as well as Chairman of the IUCN/SSC South Asian Reptile and Amphibian Specialist Group. Besides biogeography, he is interested in taxonomy and systematics of living amphibians and reptiles, fossil turtles, conservation biology, and community ecology. His other books include *Indian Turtles: A Field Guide* (1985); *Colour Guide to the Turtles and Tortoises of the Indian Subcontinent* (1991); *The World of Turtles and Crocodiles* (with Rom and Zai Whitaker, 1993); *The Turtles and Tortoises of India* (1995) and *The Animal Biodiversity of Borneo* (with Joe Charles, in preparation).

ACKNOWLEDGMENTS

A large number of colleagues helped in the compilation of the checklist with their comments and/or by providing literature: Aaron M. Bauer, Wolfgang Böhme, Anslem de Silva, Mohammed Sharif Khan, Arnold G. Kluge, Anita Malhotra, Klaus-Dieter Schulz, Garth Underwood and Romulus Whitaker.

For permission and assistance in examination of museum specimens and/or providing lists, I thank Charles Myers, Darrell Frost and David Dickey (American Museum of Natural History), Alan Stimson and Colin McCarthy (Natural History Museum, London), Jens Vindum (California Academy of Sciences), Harold K. Voris (Field Museum of Natural History), M. Rahman (Bangladesh National Museum), D. P. Sanyal and B. Dutta Gupta (Zoological Survey of India, Calcutta), R. S. Pillai and T. S. N. Murthy (Zoological Survey of India, Madras), J. R. Alfred and R. Mathew (Zoological Survey of India, Shillong), Wolfgang Böhme and Ursula Bott (Alexander Koenig Museum, Bonn), Konrad Klemmer (Natur-Museum and Forschungs-Institute Senckenberg, Frankfurt/Main), Romulus Whitaker and Harry Andrews (Madras Crocodile Bank Trust, Madras), Heinz Grillisch and Gerald Benyr (Naturhistorisches Museum, Vienna), S. Steiner and Heinz Weissinger (Niederösterreiches Landmuseum, Vienna), Tom Kemp (Oxford University Zoological Museum, Oxford), Greg Schneider (Museum of Zoology, University of Michigan, Ann Arbor) and Alain Dubois, Roger Bour, and Michel Thireau (Musée National d'Histoire Naturelle, Paris).

Museum and field research and manuscript preparation were supported by the British Council, Fauna and Flora Preservation Society, Inlaks Foundation, Madras Crocodile Bank Trust, Universiti Brunei Darussalam, World Wide Fund for Nature, and the World Conservation Union. Peter Ashton, Walter Erdelen, V. Meher-Homji, Lynne Parenti, Peter Paul Van Dijk, Robert Voeks, and Romulus Whitaker read earlier drafts of the manuscript and offered useful comments. It goes without saying that any mistakes that remain are my own.

Chapter 1

INTRODUCTION

South Asia supports a highly diverse and distinct reptile fauna, the high taxon richness figure following from the large area, covering *circa* 4.36 million square kilometres, and its situation at the crossroads of two distinctive biogeographic realms, the Palaearctic and the Oriental. Responsive to the considerable climatic and physiographic variability, habitats range from coral reefs, mangrove swamps and closed-canopy rain forests to thorn scrub vegetation and deserts. The region also includes several extreme environments, including the highest mountain and wettest location on earth.

South Asia includes Bangladesh, Bhutan, India, Maldives, Nepal, Pakistan, and Sri Lanka (Figure 1). Elsewhere, this region is referred to as the Indo-Pakistan subcontinent, the Indian subcontinent, and the Indian region. With formidable geographic barriers impeding faunal movement, including oceans, mountains, and flood plains, the region represents a distinct biogeographic unit (*cf.* Ripley and Beehler, 1990).

The treatises of Smith (1931; 1935; 1943) continue to be the authoritative sources for identification of the subcontinent's reptile fauna, despite being over half a century old. A number of squamates, especially lizards, have been described since. Murthy (1985) attempted to list all valid species then known. His work, besides containing a number of errors and omissions, includes no analysis of distributional patterns and is restricted to India. Thanks to organisations (including the Bombay Natural History Society, Herpetological Laboratory at Rabwah, Madras Crocodile Bank Trust, Wildlife Institute of India, Zoological Survey of India, Zoological Survey Department of Pakistan, as well as numerous universities in the subcontinent) and a number of European and American colleagues, our knowledge of the distribution of reptiles is considerably more refined than during Smith's time.

Biogeographic analyses of the herpetofauna, mostly for individual countries within the subcontinent, have been attempted: Mahendra (1939) and Jayaram (1974) for south Asia, Biswas and Sanyal (1980) for the Bay Islands, Swan and Leviton (1962) for Nepal, Minton (1966) for Pakistan, de Silva (1990) for Sri Lanka, and Bauer and Günther (1992) for Bhutan. In the present work, I have drawn on these and other sources for the distributional data used, although not necessarily agreeing with these workers on the interpretation.

During publication of this text, several omissions came to my attention. These, along with new records for the region, are listed below:

1. Arnold and Leviton (1977) removed *Scincus mitranus* J. Anderson, 1871, from the fauna of Pakistan, arguing convincingly that the record from Sindh is probably based on trade animals.

2. Kluge (1993b) revived *Cyrtodactylus* for the bent-toed geckos listed here in the genus *Gonydactylus*.

3. Deraniyagala (1953) described *Hemidactylus brookii parvimaculatus* from Sri Lanka, considered by Kluge (1993b) to be valid.

4. My recent work on the herpetofauna of the Nicobar Islands shows that endemicity is higher than previously assumed, and several new species of amphibians and reptiles will shortly be described. This includes a *Gekko* (which will result in the removal of *G. smithii* from the south Asian fauna), a new *Lipinia* (previously identified as *L. quadrivittatum*) and a new *Cyrtodactylus* (thought conspecific with *C. rubidus* of the Andamans). The *Dibamus* from the Nicobars differs in a number of features from *D. leucurus*, and an old name available for the Nicobarese populations will be resurrected in the future.

5. Tikader and Sharma (1992) added two species of *Phrynocephalus* to the fauna of India: *P. reticulatus* (from Ladakh) and *P. euptilophus* (from western Rajasthan).

6. Auffenberg and Rehman (1995) showed *Calotes versicolor nigrigularis* Auffenberg & Rehman (1993) to be a junior primary homonym of *Calotes nigrigularis* Ota & Hikida, 1991, from Borneo, and proposed the trinomial *Calotes versicolor farooqi* for the Pakistani lizard.

7. Zhao (as Djao) in Djao and Jiang (1977) described *Trimeresurus medoensis* from southeast Xizang (Tibet), China, northern India and Myanmar.

8. Huang's (1982) *Trimeresurus tibetanus*, described from "Chokesumo, Nyalam Co., Xizang (Tibet) Autonomous Region, China, 3,200 meters", which is apparently the species Fleming and Fleming (1973) reported (as *Trimeresurus stejnegeri*) from Nepal. I thank Patrick David for drawing my attention to this record.

9. Obst (1983) revived *Daboia* and included *Vipera russelii* and *Vipera lebetina*.

10. Webb (1995) restricted *Pelochelys bibroni* to southern New Guinea and made available the name *Pelochelys cantorii* for populations of the giant Asian softshell turtle from the Indian subcontinent and other continental and associated insular regions of Asia.

Chapter 2

METHODS

Table 1 was compiled from the literature and from museum specimens, and was sent to many colleagues (see Acknowledgments) for comments. The cut-off date for literature search and museum work was the end of 1993.

Coefficients of Community (Cj) between the physiographic zones were estimated using Jaccard's (1908) Index:

$$Cj = j/(a + b - j)$$

where, j = number of species in common between the two regions;
a = number of species in region A; and
b = number of species in region B.

Cj values range from 0 (no overlap or complete faunal dissimilarity) to 1 (total overlap or entirely similar fauna).

Cheetham and Hazel (1969) describe the properties of the coefficient that is sometimes referred to as Jaccard's measure (*e.g.*, Magurran, 1988). Marine (Dermochelyidae, Cheloniidae and Hydrophiidae) and estuarine (*Batagur, Pelochelys, Acrochordus, Cantoria, Cerberus, Fordonia* and *Gerardia*) taxa (except *Crocodylus porosus*, which may occur in both estuaries and freshwater) have been excluded from these analyses, although included in the checklist.

Cluster analysis to examine faunal relationships (generic similarity) between the physiographic zones was performed using the software SYSTAT, Version 5.03 (Wilkinson, 1990).

Source material is the checklist presented as Table 1. The list has been largely compiled from literature, from material personally examined in various museums in America, Asia, and Europe, as well as printouts of the holdings of several North American collections. Distributional records of individual species that were suspect and could not be verified were omitted. Along with the amphibians of the Republic of India (reviewed by Inger and Dutta, 1986), information available on the taxonomy, distribution, and ecology of the region's reptile fauna is far from adequate for conservation needs. Major changes in the faunal list can be expected, including the addition of new species, range corrections (especially extensions), and the recognition of sibling species within widely distributed taxa that are currently recognised as a single species (*cf.* Marx, 1988; Wüster and Thorpe, 1989).

But what exactly are species? Using Simpson's (1961) Evolutionary Species Concept (ESC), species are an "ancestral-descendent sequence of populations evolving separately from others and with its own unitary role and tendencies," as opposed to Mayr's (1942; 1963, and in subsequent works) Biological Species Concept (BSC), which defines species as groups of actually or potentially interbreeding natural populations reproductively isolated from other such groups. BSC has been challenged both by ornithologists (*e.g.*, McKitrick and Zink, 1988) and herpetologists (*e.g.*, Frost and Hillis, 1990), the primary flaw with this concept being that it is not historical (phylogenetic), and classifications based on reproductive compatibility are often inconsistent with the recovered history of evolution (Frost *et al.*, 1992).

If the rules of ESC are applied to the reptile fauna of south Asia, it would almost certainly increase the species list considerably. Some of the currently recognised subspecies, especially squamates of the continental island of Sri Lanka, will be elevated to the rank of species. Clearly, this promises to be a decade of great turmoil in the taxonomic arrangement of many groups of organisms worldwide. With further study, several taxa may not hold out even as valid subspecies (see for instance the fate of the subspecies of *Vipera russelii* from the Indian subcontinent in Wüster *et al.*, 1992). On the other hand, subspecific status has already been shown to be more appropriate for some long-established species (*e.g.*, the species of *Echis* from the subcontinent described in Auffenberg and Rehman, 1991). Here I adopt a conservative stance in unresolved cases. This work is thus an interim snap-shot of current taxonomic opinions and distributional information.

With the rapidly changing nomenclature and the continual accretion of species to the fauna, a few remarks on the nomenclature used are warranted. I have followed King and Burke (1989), Das (1991) and Iverson (1992a) for turtles (the term "turtle" will be used hereafter to refer to the entire Order Testudines). For squamates, the scheme of Smith (1935; 1943) has been followed, superimposed by more recent studies on particular taxa, including Kluge (1991; 1993b) for gekkonids, Arnold (1992) and Moody (1980) for agamids, Mittleman (1952) for lygosomine scincids, Gans (1966) for uropeltids, Kluge (1993a) for erycines, Gyi (1970), Lazell *et al.* (1991), Savage (1952), Malnate (1960), Malnate and Underwood (1988), among others, for colubrids; and Kharin (1984) for hydrophiids. I have used Burger's (1971) new genus (*Ovophis*) of crotalids, made available by Hoge and Romano (1981): see Smith (1989). Because of space constraints, I shall refrain from commenting at length on the recent reallocation of individual species. A synopsis of the reptiles of the south Asian region, comprising valid names, synonymy, information on primary types, distribution, and references is in preparation.

Chapter 3

PHYSIOGRAPHIC ZONES

Physiographic zones within the south Asian region used include:
1. The northern islands of the Bay Islands group, including the Andamans;
2. The southern islands of the Bay Islands group, including the Nicobars;

Figure 1. Map of south Asia showing the physiographical zones and their presumed boundaries.

3. Deccan and plains of northern India, hereafter referred to as "Deccan" (peninsular India minus the area included in the Western and Eastern Ghats, plus northern India, excluding the Himalayas, the Northwest and the Northeast);
4. Eastern Ghats (hills of southeastern India and associated plains to the east);
5. Himalayas (northern Uttar Pradesh, Nepal, Bhutan, Sikkim and northern West Bengal);
6. Northeast (northeastern India, northeastern and southwestern Bangladesh);
7. Northwest (northwestern India and the plains of Pakistan);
8. The continental island of Sri Lanka;
9. Trans-Himalayas (northern and western Pakistan and Jammu and Kashmir, separated from the Himalayas by the Sutlej river);
10. Western Ghats (hills of southwestern India and associated plains to the west);

General description of vegetation and physiographic features of south Asia can be found in Champion and Seth (1968), Collins *et al.* (1991), Fernando (1968), Mani (1974a), and Monga and Sahgal (1990).

The principal physical and biological features of the physiographic zones shown in Figure 1 are briefly described below.

1, 2. BAY ISLANDS (AN, NI)

The Andaman and Nicobar archipelago is situated between 5° 40'N and 92° 10'E, in the Bay of Bengal, the two groups separated by the 10° Channel. These islands form a chain of submarine mountains that sprawl in a crescent between Cape Negrais in Myanmar to Achin Head in Sumatra, Indonesia. The total land area of these islands is an estimated 8,293 km², including a larger Andamans group (6,340 km²) and the much smaller Nicobars (1,953 km²). Average annual rainfall exceeds 3,000 mm, and the great variety of habitats, including bays, coral reefs, mangrove, and rainforests on hill ranges that reach 700 m, support a species-rich herpetofauna.

As much as ten percent of the flora of these islands is endemic including 225 species of vascular plants. The human population on these islands is presently over 300,000. Over 33,000 tourists visited the Bay Islands in 1990, the high human presence leading to pollution and destruction of marine and land plant life (Sinha, 1992). The biology and threats to living resources of the Andamans have been discussed by Whitaker (1985).

The herpetofauna of the Andamans is an impoverished one from Myanmar, these islands being a part of the Tennasserim range of mountains, while that of the Nicobars, an oceanic group (P. Ashton, *pers. comm.*, 1993), is allied to that of Sumatra, presumably being established by overwater (waif) dispersal. Important reviews of the nonmarine herpetofauna of the Andamans and Nicobars include those of Annandale (1904, 1905), Smith (1940), Whitaker (1978), and Biswas and Sanyal (1977a; 1980).

3. DECCAN (DC)

The flat country that comprises peninsular India, excluding the hill ranges to the east and west, and south of the areas watered by the Himalayan rivers, has been referred to as the Deccan, a region of considerable aridity. Until the Miocene-Pliocene, evergreen forests were widespread in peninsular India, as indicated by palaeontological evidence. Ripley *et al.* (1987) argued for the existence of a "humid south Asian forest biota" even during the Late Pleistocene, covering much of the Indian region, including the Deccan. The conversion of these wet forests to deciduous forests is possibly an effect of the decline in rainfall, a result of the slight southern shift of the equator, the uplift of the Himalayas (but see Paterson, 1993 for an alternative viewpoint) and the rise of the Western Ghats (Meher-Homji, 1990), although human activities over the past 10,000 years must have also contributed to the change.

Nonetheless, a great variety of vegetation is represented. The following phytogeographic regions are from Meher-Homji (1990):

1. *Shorea-Cleistanthus collinus-Croton oblongifolius* type, in the northeast.
2. *Shorea-Buchanania-Cleistanthus* type, in central and south.
3. *Shorea-Syzygium operculatum-Toona ciliata-Symplocos spicata* type, in the north.
4. *Toona-Garuga* type, in the east-central.
5. *Hardwickia binata* type, to the south.
6. *Anogeissus pendula* type, to the northwest, and
7. *Acacia senegal-Angoeissus pendula* type, to the northwest.

Additional sources of information on the plant geography of the Deccan include Mani (1974b), Gadgil and Meher-Homji (1990), and Champion and Seth (1968).

Few concerted attempts have been made to survey the Deccan for its herpetofauna, despite it accessibility. Sanyal and Dasgupta (1990) surveyed the Bastar region of south-central India, and produced an inventory that shows no endemics.

4. EASTERN GHATS (EG)

The Eastern Ghats represent a weathered relict of the peninsular plateau, marked by a series of low isolated hills that run from the Khondmal Hills in the Baudh-Khandmal (Pulbani) District, Orissa State, southwards to central Tamil Nadu State, where it veers off towards the southwest to meet the Western Ghats (see below) in the Nilgiris. At 1,750 m, the Biligirirangan Hills is the highest peak in the region. The northern and southern sections of the Eastern Ghats are separated by the Godavari delta, which is approximately 130 km in width, other important breaks including the rivers Mahanadi and Krishna. The southern subzone is drier, with dry deciduous and thorn scrub, while the northern part is relatively mesic with dry and moist deciduous forests. General description of the region can be found in Krishna Raju and Subba Rao (1990), Krishna Raju et al. (1987), Legris and Meher-Homji (1982), and Subba Rao et al. (1982).

The dominant vegetation type is dry-deciduous, with patches of moist-deciduous and semi-evergreen forests. *Shola*-type and treeless zones are common only at high elevations. Herpetological diversity is higher than in the Deccan, but substantially lower than of the Western Ghats. Extensive deforestation of the natural forests, slash-and-burn agriculture, poaching, encroachment, mining, and monoculture plantations have reduced the quality of the natural vegetation and its extent.

The herpetofauna has been dealt with by McCann (1945), Pillai and Murthy (1983), Sharma (1965), Daniels and Ishwar (1993), and Sanyal et al. (1993).

5. HIMALAYAS (HM)

The Himalayan mountain range includes some of the highest mountains on earth, and profoundly affects the climate and vegetation of almost the entire Indian region. Eight rivers drain from these mountains (including the Ganga, Brahmaputra, Yangtze, Indus, and Mekong), these together carrying 25% of the dissolved material that reaches the world's oceans, although the area they drain, including the plateau, is less than 5% of the earth's land area (Paterson, 1993). The Himalayas, including the Trans-Himalayas (see below) cover an area of 236,300 km^2, over parts of Pakistan, India, Nepal and Bhutan, and include a variety of vegetation, from moist deciduous, through subtropical broad-leaved forests, to coniferous, mixed coniferous and alpine scrub forests. Included in the region are the *terai*, a swampy belt of maximum width 13 km, the *bhabars*, which are deep, boulder deposits of maximum width 21 km, skirting the outermost hills of the Himalayas, and the *duns*, which are broad elevated valleys at *circa* 600 m altitude, at the outer range of the Himalayas.

The eastern Himalayas are wetter than the western part, receiving at least 2,000 mm of average annual rainfall, often much more. However, the winter months (November–March) are relatively dry. The monsoonal climax is in July. Secondary wet mixed forests exist in the low-lying areas of the eastern Himalayas, including the moister areas of the *terai* and the lower areas of the *bhabar*. Rainfall usually exceeds 2,500 mm a year, and the areas experience four dry months in a year. As a result of its ultravaried topography, both species diversity and endemism among plants is high, especially in many deep and semi-isolated valleys (Myers, 1988). Typical trees represented include *Michelia montana, Turpinia pomifera, Schima wallichii, Ilex godajam, Saurauja roxburghii,* and *Aporosa dioica*. Subalpine forests are represented in the western and central Himalayas, dominant vegetation being *Quercus incana* and *Q. dilatata*. Thickets of *Rhododendron hyperanthum, R. leptodotum,* and *R. pumilum* occur between 3,500–5,000 m altitude. Subtropical pine forests are recorded where temperature ranges are between 1,500–3,000 mm a year, and include *Quercus amellosa* and *Q. lineata, Rhododendron* spp., *Lyonia* spp., *Pinus roxburghii* and *P. insularis*. The absence of forests of *Pinus roxburghii* in Kashmir is considered due to the weakened southwestern monsoons (Champion and Seth, 1968).

At 4,000–5,000 m are the alpine pastures, considered grasslands although there is little grass represented, the dominant vegetation being perennial mesophytic herbs such as *Primula* spp., *Anemone* spp., *Iris* spp., and *Gentiana* spp. The vegetation of the Himalayas has been described by Rau (1974).

Levels of deforestation in the Himalayas have become severe (Numata, 1983; see also Myers, 1988, and references quoted therein). Forests of the Himalayas are being felled for demands for shifting cultivation and extensive potato cultivation. Other threats to the vegetation of the region are grazing at high altitudes and fires in the bamboo brakes.

The herpetofauna has been discussed by Agrawal (1979), Fleming and Fleming (1973), Nanhoe and Ouboter (1987), Swan and Leviton (1962), and Waltner (1975a, 1975b, 1975c, 1975d).

6. NORTHEAST (NE)

With rainfall exceeding 2,000 mm, the Northeast supports a rich tropical vegetation. The main vegetation types represented include moist deciduous, semi-evergreen and temperate montane forests, including *Lagerstroemia, tetrameles, Shorea robusta, Quercus, Juglans,* and *Magnolia*. Bamboos and grasses are specially diverse and common in both the wet and dry areas of the Northeast. Tropical evergreen forests in the region comprise forests with three-tiered structures, looming to about 46 m above the forest floor. Climatic fluctuations throughout the year are minimal, temperatures on average ranging from 20–30° C in the plains, although humidity can be as high as 80–90 percent. Descriptions of the plant life of the region can be found in Mani (1974c), Ramdas (1992), and Rao (1974).

Encroachment, felling for timber, and slash-and-burn agriculture, as well as hydroelectric projects and constructions of roads and railways, threaten the natural forests of Assam (Choudhury, 1993), the largest of the northeastern states.

Herpetological investigations in the region have been few. Mathew (1983) and Das (1988) reported on collections made from the Northeast in recent years.

7. NORTHWEST (NW)

The Northwest includes the eastern parts of Pakistan and the extreme western parts of India, and is bounded by the Indus and Nara Valleys in the west, the Aravalis in the east, and the Kutch to the south. To the north lie the Indian states of Haryana and Punjab, comprising the plains of the Sutlej and Chambal Rivers. The Thar region itself is 446,000 km² in extent. Archaeological evidence points to the fertility of the region around Mohenjo Daro, some 6,000 years before present (Mackay, 1934), where culverts carried storm water during 2,750 B.C. References to the physical and biological features of the Northwest are contained in Mani (1974c), Meher-Homji and Bharucha (1975), Roberts (1977), Singh (1978), and Gupta (1986).

The region is mostly composed of hills, stony plateaus, or peneplains. Severe winters characterize the area, which is outside the influence of the monsoons. Rainfall is 250–500 mm a year, and the mean maximum temperature over 45° C during May and June. Thorny thickets, dominated by *Acacia senegalensis, A. catechu, Prosopis cinoraria,* and *Zizyphus nummularia* are the common vegetation to be seen. The dry season lasts 8.5–10 months. Dominant tree species in the desert peneplains (annual rainfall 250 mm or less) include *Prosopis cineraria* (densities exceeding 25 trees ha⁻¹), *Zizyphus numularia,* and *Capparis decidua.* In the western parts, in the Nara region of Pakistan, the vegetation is sparse, consisting of xerophytic shrubs like *Haloxylon* spp.

Heavily grazed and logged, the vegetation is today largely degraded. Large-scale deforestation of the *deodar* trees in the upper valleys of the Sutej, Jamuna, Beas, Ravi, and Chenab Rivers during 1850–1870 for the railway industry has left the region barren (Gaston, 1990).

Minton (1966), Mertens (1969), Biswas and Sanyal (1977b), and Khan (1985a) have reported on the herpetofauna of the arid Northwest.

8. SRI LANKA (SL)

Sri Lanka and the Indian peninsula together constitute the tectonic structure known as the Deccan Plate. The wet zone of Sri Lanka represents the only aseasonal area between Malesia and the eastern coast of Madagascar (Ashton and Gunatilleke, 1987).

The 65,000 km^2 continental island of Sri Lanka (formerly Ceylon) is generally divided into three climatic zones:

a. Low-country dry zone, including the northern half and the east,

b. Low-country wet zone, including the southwest; and

c. Montane zone, including the centre of the southern half of the island.

Sri Lanka's connection to the mainland, for the first time during the Miocene and many times subsequently (Cooray, 1967), has lead to the invasion of many species of distinctly Indian origin, although endemicity in the herpetofauna is also high. Jansen and De Zoysa (1992) showed that Sri Lanka has greater biodiversity per unit area than any other Asian country, this being concentrated to the mesic southwestern lowlands and the central highlands.

General accounts of the region including its physical and climatic features and the biota can be found in Erdelen (1989) and Hoffman (1990).

Reduction in Sri Lanka's forest cover between 1900 and 1988 has been estimated to be from 70% to about 20%, major causal factors being logging for timber, for settlement and agriculture, and the expansion of tourism (Preu and Erdelen, 1992). At present, natural forest covers about 30% of the dry zone and 9% of the wet zone (Erdelen, 1993).

Sri Lanka has had the attention of a number of active herpetologists: Deraniyagala (1953), P. H. D. H. de Silva (1980), A. de Silva (1990), and Taylor (1950, 1953).

9. TRANS-HIMALAYAS (TH)

The Zanskar, Ladakh, and Karakorum dominate the landscape of the Trans-Himalayas (outer Himalayas). To the east, the Zanskar and Ladakh reaches down to the Tibetan plateau, the region marked with brackish marshes and bogs. Included in the region is a large (1,180 km^2) glacier, the Siachen, the largest outside the polar regions. Within the Trans-Himalayas, Ladakh, with an area of 97,782 km^2, is worthy of comment. The region is composed of mountains that are up to 6,600 m and sandy valleys drained by the Indus. The sedimentary deposits are mostly marine in origin, and are up to Late Tertiary in age. The dry climate is due in part to the low temperature (below 0° C) that inhibits absorption of water by roots of plants during the winter and early spring when occasional showers take place.

The vegetation of the Trans-Himalayas include subtropical evergreen and coniferous forests as well as alpine steppe. In general, the rainfall increases along a west-east gradient, from 500 mm in Peshawar, Pakistan, to 1,000 in the Kumaon, Uttar Pradesh, in India. At higher altitudes, vegetation is xerophytic, dominated by *Salix denticulata, Juniperus communis, Mertensia tibetica,* and *Potentilla desertorum*. The alpine steppe vegetation shows high endemism. The vegetation of the Ladakh region has been described by Sapru and Kachroo (1979).

Growing numbers of pastoralists and their livestock, logging, and tourism are factors that threaten this unique and fragile world.

Important papers dealing with the herpetofauna of the region include those of Acharji and Kripalani (1951), Minton (1966), Duda and Sahi (1977), Gruber (1981), Murthy and Sharma (1976), and Murthy *et al.* (1979).

10. WESTERN GHATS (WG)

The southwest Indian forests along with those of southwestern Sri Lanka comprise the western-most outliers of the Indo-Malaysian Formation of the tropical moist forest (Richards, 1953). The Western Ghats run along the west coast of peninsular India 50–100 km inland and are a series of hill ranges often isolated from each other by flat savanna. The region extends from the central part of present day Maharashra state (where a modified type of evergreen forest survives) to the southern parts of Tamil Nadu and Kerala, including the hill ranges of the Nilgiris, Annamalais, and the Palnis, where hill ranges reach altitudes of 450–1500 m and receive average and annual rainfall in excess of 2,000 mm.

Typical flora of the Western Ghats include *Lagerstroemia lanceolata*, *Dalbergia latifolia*, *Toona ciliata*, and *Chukrassia tabularis*. Details of the Western Ghats, including its physiography and climate, can be found in Subramanyam and Nayar (1974) and Pascal (1988).

An important review of the herpetofauna of the region is that of Groombridge (1990), which predicted that as many as 150 species of amphibians and reptiles will prove to the endemic to the region. Collections from the Western Ghats have been made by numerous workers, including Inger *et al.* (1984), Das and Whitaker (1990), Malhotra and Davis (1991), and Murthy (1986).

The physiographic zones within India in this work are similar to those in Inger and Dutta (1986). The oceanic archipelago to the west of the Indian peninsula known as the Maldives, and the Indian Union Territory of Lakshadweep (formerly Laccadives) have been omitted, because these have no native species of reptiles.

Chapter 4

RESULTS AND DISCUSSION

4.1. BIODIVERSITY AND ENDEMICITY

The 632 species of reptiles recorded from south Asia (Table 1) belong to three orders, 25 families, and 185 genera. The fauna is particularly rich in turtles of the family Bataguridae (16 species); lizards of the families Gekkonidae (97 species), Agamidae (68 species), Scincidae (87 species); and snakes of the families Typhlopidae (23 species), Uropeltidae (47 species), Colubridae (176 species), Elapidae (16 species), Hydrophiidae (21 species) and Viperidae (25 species).

The accretion of species description to the fauna is shown in five-year intervals in Figure 2. A very large number of species have been described between 1850 and 1880. However, it is the activities of a single herpetologist, based at the Natural History Museum, London (then British Museum [Natural History]), over a period of several decades that explain the great additions to the fauna. John Edward Gray (1800–1875) added many species to the reptile fauna of the Indian region. Between 1827 and 1872, Gray described 54 species that are presently considered valid, including 14 Indian freshwater turtles. These figures are excluding six reptile species Gray described in collaboration with Thomas Hardwicke. Gray is also credited with the hiring of Albert Günther (1830–1914), who, between 1858 and 1881, described 60 reptiles species that are still valid, and in turn, employed George A. Boulenger (1858–1937), who between 1885 and 1918 described 37 species from this region that are still considered valid. The three aforementioned herpetologists are thus together responsible for describing a quarter of the subcontinent's reptile fauna.

The two world wars have had negative effects on the productivity of herpetologists worldwide (Gans, 1992). In south Asia, relatively few species of reptiles were described between the beginning of the First World War and the period subsequent to the Second World War and the time of independence of these former British colonies, till about the 1970's decade, when a revival appears to have taken place (Figure 2).

Eleven species have been described in the first three years of the 1990's decade, indicating a revival of interest in south Asia's reptile fauna. Clearly many new species will be added to the subcontinent's reptile fauna with more

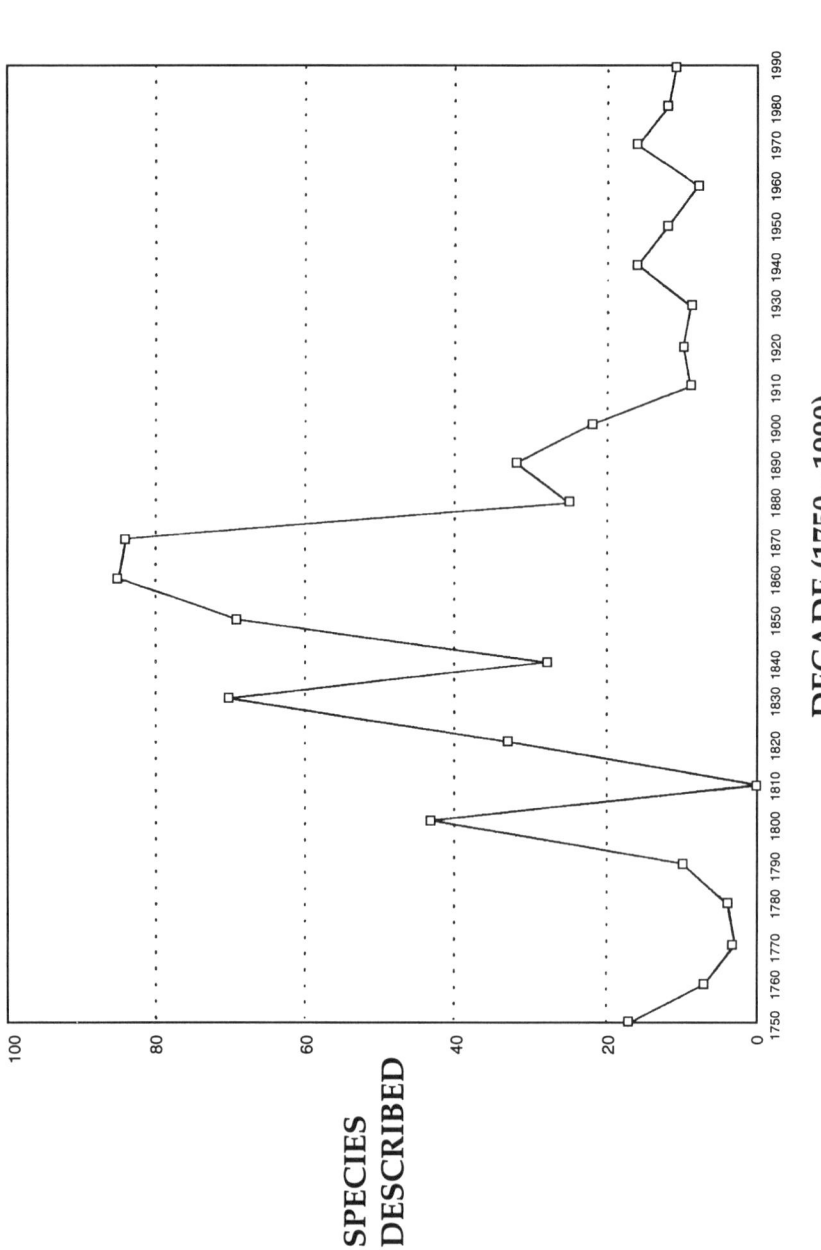

Figure 2. The accretion of species at present considered valid to the reptile fauna of south Asia in 10-year intervals.

intensive fieldwork, especially in the regions rich in reptile biodiversity, including the Northeast, Eastern and Western Ghats, and the virtually unsurveyed outliers west of the Himalayas. At the time of writing, several new species and subspecies or new records of species for south Asia have been reported by colleagues or discovered during fieldwork personally undertaken. These include:

1. A new uropeltid from the Western Ghats (Carl Gans, *pers. comm.*, 1990),
2. A new gecko of the genus *Hemidactylus* from Nepal (Gerald Benyr, *pers. comm.*, 1992),
3. Two possibly new species of lizards from Sri Lanka's Matara district (S. Ranatunga, *in litt.* to Simon Stuart, 1992),
4. Several new species of agamids of the *Stellio* group from northern Pakistan (W. Böhme, *pers. comm.* 1992),
5. A new species of natricine from the Western Ghats (R. Whitaker and I. Das, unpublished),
6. A new species of roofed turtle of the genus *Kachuga* from northeastern India (I. Das, unpublished),
7. A new subspecies of roofed turtle of the *Kachuga* group from Bangladesh and northeastern India (I. Das, unpublished).

Additionally, as already discussed, application of ESC would increase the number of species dramatically.

Endemicity at the species level is high: 304 species are restricted to one of the 10 physiographic zones, and an additional 98 species occur in more than one zone but not extralimitally (*i.e.*, outside the south Asian region). The total endemicity at the species level is thus 402 (or 63.7%). Twenty-two genera are endemic to a single region within the subcontinent, and 16 occur in more than one zone, but not extralimitally. The total number of genera restricted to the region is 38. *Mabuya* and *Oligodon* are genera with endemic species in the greatest number of zones (seven and five, respectively), compared to all other genera, these having a total of 20 and 23 species, respectively in the subcontinent. The endemic genus *Uropeltis* from Sri Lanka, the Western Ghats, and almost peripherally from the Eastern Ghats, has the most number of species (23). A total of 19 endemic genera are monotypic. Sri Lanka has the highest number of endemic genera (10), followed by the Western Ghats (6) and the Northeast (2). These zones also contain many endemic species (Table 3). As expected, species endemicity is strongly correlated to species diversity (Figure 3; $r = 0.794$; $P < 0.05$), indicating that more endemic species are likely to occur in areas with greater species richness.

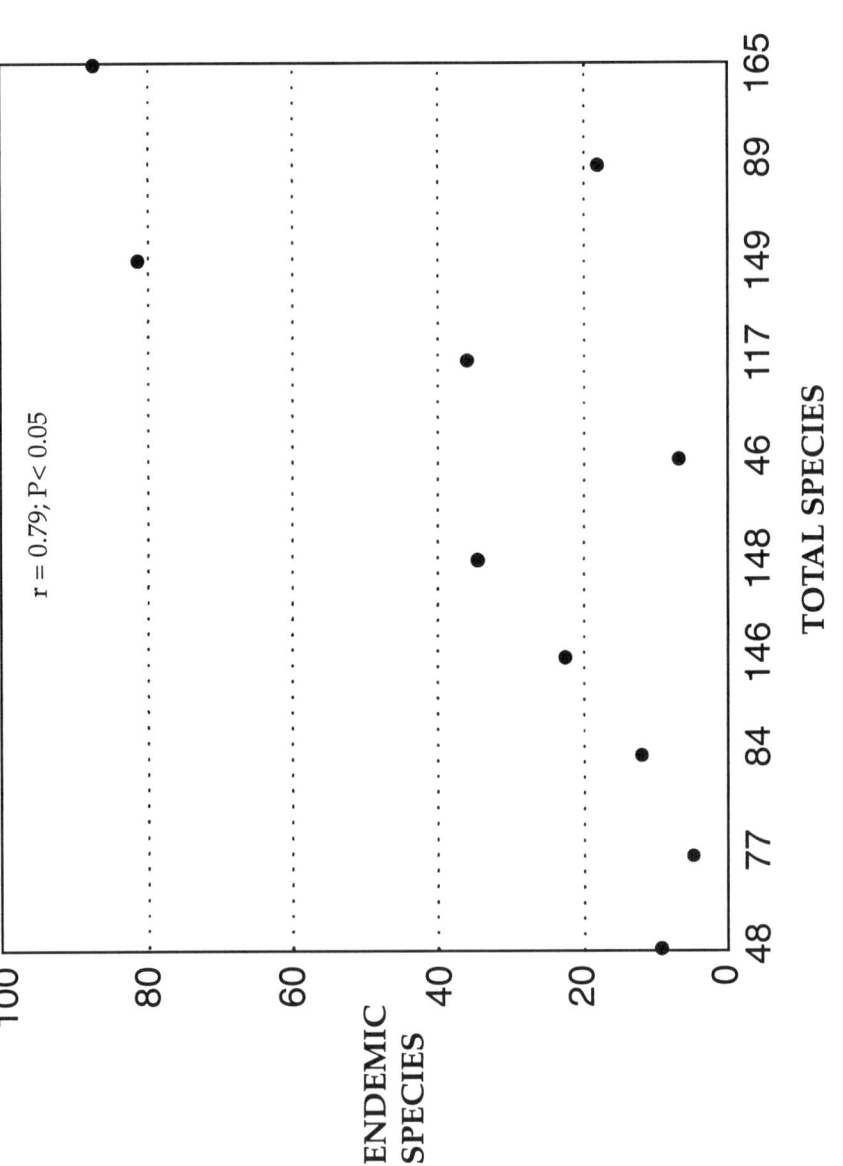

Figure 3. Relationship between species diversity and species endemicity in the 10 physiographic zones of south Asia.

Thirteen genera, none of which is monotypic, are found in all 10 zones. However, often just one species in the genus is widespread. These include: *Hemidactylus frenatus* (except Northeast and Trans-Himalayas), *Calotes versicolor* (except Nicobars), *Mabuya macularia* (except Andaman and Nicobar), *Varanus bengalensis* (except Andaman and Nicobars), *Ramphotyphlops braminus, Boiga trigonata* (except Andaman and Nicobars), *Dendrelaphis tristis* (except Northeast, Andaman and Nicobars), *Xenochrophis piscator* (except Andaman and Nicobar), *Bungarus caerulea* (except Nicobars, Western Ghats, Northeast and Trans-Himalayas), *Elaphe helena, Lycodon aulicus, Oligodon arnensis, Naja naja* (for the last four species, all zones except Northwest, Northeast, Andaman and Nicobars). Some of these widespread genera include species that are frequently human-commensals, including several house geckos of the genus *Hemidactylus*. Others commonly live in the proximity of human habitations and/or are associated with disturbed areas such as secondary forests and agricultural fields (*e.g.*, the rodent-eating *Naja naja* and *Varanus bengalensis*). Clearly, human activities have increased the ranges of many of these widespread and presumably adaptable species by creating new niches.

Distinctive radiation is shown by several endemic reptile genera in the Indian region (Table 4). Examples include *Aspideretes* (four species, widespread within the mainland), *Ristella* (4 species from the Western Ghats), *Lankascincus* (6 species from Sri Lanka), *Nessia* (8 species from Sri Lanka), *Rhinophis* (12 species from the Western Ghats and Sri Lanka), *Uropeltis* (23 species from the Western Ghats and Sri Lanka, two Western Ghat species co-occurring in the Eastern Ghats) and *Aspidura* (6 species from Sri Lanka). Only a few genera have more species within the Indian subcontinent than extralimitally. For example, the genus *Bungarus* has eight species within the region, and only 4 in southeast Asia, which do not occur in the Indian region, suggesting that south Asia is the centre of origin of the group. Other examples of distinctly Indian radiation include the genera *Kachuga*: 6 species in south Asia, one in Myanmar, and *Lissemys*: one widespread species in the Indian region, one in a peripheral zone (Myanmar).

Many genera have members distributed over the boundaries of the Indian region. These genera have been labeled "transitional," since no faunal links could be ascertained, these taxa distributed along or close to the boundaries of the Indian region. Fourteen of the 23 transitional genera occur in the Himalayas, more than in any other zones.

4.2. FAUNAL CHARACTERISTICS OF PHYSIOGRAPHIC ZONES

Until the Early Jurassic, peninsular India was part of the Gondwanaland supercontinent. Approximately 140 million years before present, the peninsula separated from the supercontinent and began to drift towards the northern hemisphere. The collision of the Indian peninsula with the Tibeto-Assam-Myanmar region, which created the Himalayan massif and much of the physiographic diversity that characterizes the region (see Whitmore, 1987), took place approximately 38 million years before present (Molnar and Tapponier, 1975). In general, the land, ecology, and its plant and animal life has been influenced by a variety of abiotic and biotic factors, including the invasion by Palaearctic and Oriental species, the proximity of the Himalayas and its outliers that have stopped or impeded the movement of many species, and the marked seasonality of rainfall caused by the monsoons. Human occupancy, particularly in the last millennium, also has had a major influence on the abundance and distribution of the region's biota.

In this section, the faunal characteristics of each physiographic zone are examined.

1, 2. Bay Islands (AN, NI)

The Andamans group consists of 291 islands, the Nicobars of 28, both groups located in the Bay of Bengal. Floristically, the group of islands collectively referred to as the Andamans are similar to the Tenasserim coast of Myanmar, and Ripley and Beehler (1989) hypothesized that these islands may have been contiguous with the mainland during the Late Pleistocene, 18,000 years before present, when sea levels dropped (see Section 4.5). This argument is supported by the presence of dipterocarp trees (P. Ashton, *pers. comm.*, 1993) on the Andamans. On the other hand, the Nicobars appear to be a group of truly oceanic islands, with no dipterocarps, its biota presumably being established by over-water dispersal.

Nicobar's avifauna has been shown to be an impoverished subset of that of the Andamans by Ripley and Beehler (1989), who contended that drops in sea levels during the Pleistocene failed to join the two island groups because of the deep saltwater strait (the 10° Channel) between the two island groups.

A comparison of the reptile fauna of the two island groups fails to detect any major taxonomic differences that can be correlated to island type, *i.e.*, the faunas of continental versus that of oceanic islands. Crowell's (1986) study of mammals on the islands in the Gulf of Maine shows that landbridge islands support more species, but not different species, from those found on oceanic islands in the same region.

That there is just one endemic agamid genus on the Bay Islands, *Coryphophylax*, may reflect the relatively recent colonization by the reptile fauna by over-water dispersion. The primary colonization source for these islands is thought to be Myanmar (for the Andamans) and Thailand (for the Nicobars; see below). However, the centre of origin of the gekkonid *Phelsuma andamanense* remains unknown. The 31 other species belonging to the genus (Kluge, 1991) are distributed over small oceanic islands in the Indian Ocean, with about half the species occurring on Madagascar. Another southeast Asian element is *Lipinia* (two species on the Bay Islands, *L. macrotympanum* and *L. quadrivittatum*), the other members of the genus being widespread in the Sundas, New Guinea, and the Philippines.

The Andamans have 11 reptile species endemic to the Bay Islands, while the Nicobars have 13, the two island groups sharing 6 endemic species (Das, in prep.). In all, 22 (including ten exclusively endemic) species that occur in the Andamans have not been found on the Nicobars, while the Nicobars also have 21 (including 7 exclusively endemic) species that have thus far not been reported from the Andamans. The deep 10° Channel that runs between the two island groups is a barrier between the ranges of endemic avian species of both the Andamans and the Nicobars (Ripley and Beehler, 1989). In all, 70 species of nonmarine reptiles have been recorded from the two island groups.

Indo-Malayan fauna dominates in the Bay Islands, comprising 19 genera on the Nicobars and 15 on the Andamans (Table 6). These islands also have a species of the genus *Lepidodactylus*, whose closest relatives are distributed around the Philippines, as well as 2 Tibeto-Yunnanese genera (*Cuora* and *Gekko*). Only 3 distinctly Indian genera, *Bungarus*, *Calotes*, and *Hemidactylus*, occur on these islands.

3. Deccan (DC)

The Deccan, here also including the plains of north-central India, is composed of a series of upland valleys and extensive plains, intersected by small to large rivers. For its large land surface, the Deccan appear remarkably impoverished in terms of endemic species: three species of endemic lizards and two endemic snakes occur here, with no endemic genera of either. In general, the zone also is depauperate in reptile species diversity, with a mere 77 species recorded, the lowest among the physiographic zones on the mainland.

Extralimital faunal links in this region include the Turkomanian-Central Asian genus *Laudakia* (only in the extreme north), besides 8 Afro-Mediterranean genera, including *Chamaeleo*, *Echis*, *Eryx*, *Eublepharis*, *Geochelone*, *Ophisops*, *Pristurus*, *Vipera*, and surprisingly, one that has not been hitherto reported from the intervening regions, *Coronella* (Table 5). A single Tibeto-Yunnanese genus, *Eumeces*, occurs in the Deccan. Indo-Malayan elements are represented by seven genera. The Deccan, however, is rich in genera that are Indian radiation: *Ahaetulla, Bungarus, Calotes, Hemidactylus, Kachuga, Lissemys, Melanochelys, Spalerosophis,* and *Teratolepis*.

4. Eastern Ghats (EG)

The Eastern Ghats, at present much altered through anthropogenic changes, has endemics at the generic (2) and specific (12) levels. Both endemic genera (*Barkudia* and *Sepsophis*) contain monotypic fossorial skink species. In all, 84 species have been reported from the region.

Extralimital elements in the Eastern Ghats include 7 Afro-Mediterranean genera, and a single Tibeto-Yunnanese genus, but as many as 14 Indo-Malayan genera (Table 5).

5. Himalayas (HM)

The Himalayas have a single endemic genus (*Elachistodon*), a total of 146 species, of which 22 are endemic (including three belonging to the genus *Japalura*). The highest overlap between the physiographic zones in the Indian region is shown by the Himalayas and the Northeast, with as many as 48 co-occurring genera in these two zones.

Extralimital elements in the Himalayas include four Tibeto-Yunnanese elements, and eleven Indo-Malayan elements. Noteworthy is that no Turko-manian-Central Asian or Afro-Mediterranean genera are represented (Tables 5 and 6). Eight of 12 genera that are Indian radiations are represented in the Himalayas.

6. Northeast (NE)

The Northeast presents an interesting case. It has 2 endemic genera (both lizards) and 35 (out of a total of 148) endemic species, including 2 turtles, the only zone in the subcontinent, besides the Western Ghats and the Himalayas, with its own turtles. Interestingly, both endemic genera of saurians (*Mictopholis* and *Oriocalotes*) are monotypic. Both the turtles *Kachuga sylhetensis* and *Aspideretes nigricans* clearly belong to the Indian fauna, the other members of their genera being distributed further west.

The fauna of the Northeast is largely Indo-Malayan: 23 genera from the region have more species in the hilly country of southeast Asia than elsewhere. There are no genera of western Palaearctic affinities. The Northeast does have 10 of the 12 genera that are Indian radiation, besides its own endemics referred to earlier. The total number of transitional genera is 17.

7. Northwest (NW)

Turkomanian-Central Asian and Afro-Mediterranean elements dominate in the Northwest (see Table 6). The region has 117 species, 36 of which are endemic. Although endemicity is not particularly high at the generic level, many genera, especially of gekkonid lizards, are unrepresented elsewhere in the subcontinent, including *Agamura* (three species), *Alsophylax* (one species), *Asiocolotes* (1 species), *Bunopus* (1 species), *Microgecko* (1 species), *Pristurus* (1 species), *Ptyodactylus* (one species), and *Tropiocolotes* (1 species).

The fauna of the Northwest is overwhelmingly Palaearctic, including 8 Turkomanian-Central Asian elements and 20 that are Afro-Mediterranean. The Northwest has 11 out of a total of 20 transitional genera.

8. Sri Lanka (SL)

The continental island of Sri Lanka, lying at the foot of the Indian peninsula, has the highest endemicity rate in its reptile fauna compared to all other physiographic zones in south Asia, even after adjusting for size of the land area. Of the 65 genera and 149 species excluding marine and estuarine species, 10 (15.4%) and 81 (54.4%), respectively, are confined to this island (Tables 3 and 4). For 2 genera (*Rhinophis* and *Hypnale*), the number of species on Sri Lanka exceeds that on the mainland. Nine of 12 species (75%) of uropeltids of the genus *Rhinophis* and 2 of 3 (66.7%) viperids of the genus *Hypnale* are confined to Sri Lanka, which suggests that the island is the centre of origin and diversification of these genera.

Endemicity among the species in Sri Lanka is high. A few of these are clearly vicariants, the Sri Lankan *Otocryptis wiegmanni* is a vicar of the mainland's *O. beddomei*, while *Calodactylodes aureus*, also from the mainland, is replaced on the island by *C. illingworthi*. If the endemic Sri Lankan subspecies of squamates are elevated to species rank following ESC, these would be considered vicars of their mainland sister species.

The extralimital elements of Sri Lanka (Table 5) show Indo-Malayan links (21 genera), as well as elements that are Afro-Mediterranean (6 genera) and Filippino (1 genus).

9. Trans-Himalayas (TH)

The Trans-Himalayas have a young and relatively specialized fauna, and contain certain postglacial Turkomanian and Central Asian elements. Eighty-nine species have been reported from the region, 19 of which are endemic. Four endemic species belong to the gekkonid genus *Cyrtopodion*.

Extralimital elements include Palaearctic (5 Turkomanian-Central Asian genera; two Afro-Mediterranean genus); plus Oriental (11 Indo-Malayan genera; four Tibeto-Yunnanese genera) elements (Table 5). The total number of transitional genera in the Trans-Himalayas is 6.

10. Western Ghats (WG)

The Western Ghats exhibits high endemicity at the species level (88 out of a total of 165 species), but surprisingly, not at the general level (five). The zone shares an additional three genera of uropeltids exclusively with Sri Lanka. Approximately half (31 species) of the Western Ghat endemics are composed of uropeltids. The other dominant genus, in terms of species numbers, is the gekkonid *Cnemaspis* with at least 12 species recorded. Kluge (1991; 1993b) lists 35 species under this genus, the members of which are widely distributed in south and southeast Asia. The absence of *Cnemaspis* in the Northeast may appear surprising, but this distributional pattern has been reported for other taxa of both amphibians and reptiles (see Section 4.7).

Extralimital links of the Western Ghat fauna are mostly Indo-Malayan, including 18 genera, although *Chalcides*, *Eryx*, *Geochelone*, *Ophisops*, and *Vipera* represent the Afro-Mediterranean fauna on these hill ranges. Eight of 12 genera that are considered Indian radiation are found here (Table 5).

4.3. PATTERNS AND CORRELATES OF DIVERSITY

The four tropical moist forest zones display high species diversity (Table 3): Sri Lanka (149), Western Ghats (165), Northeast (148), and Himalayas (146). For its large land surface, the Deccan has few species (77), but the Bay Islands are considered to be species-rich: 49 each in the Andamans and Nicobars after adjusting for their small land surface area. On the mainland, the Eastern Ghats, the Northwest and the Trans-Himalayas have the lowest reptile species diversity (84, 117 and 89, respectively).

The general pattern observed within the reptile fauna of the 10 zones is that snake species outnumber lizards in the forested zones, at least on the mainland (Himalayas, Northeast, Western Ghats) and also Sri Lanka and the Andamans, while lizards outnumber snakes in the zones with less tree cover (Northwest and Trans-Himalayas). In both the Eastern Ghats and the Deccan, which were once clad with tropical forests but are now mostly degraded, the former pattern prevails. It would appear from the above that more niches are available for snakes in tropical moist forests than in other habitats, and/or more snakes are linked to habitats with stable environmental conditions, than are lizards. Schall and Pianka (1977) found lizard faunas to be more diverse in areas with greater sunfall than other groups of amphibians and reptiles, in the Iberian peninsula, Australia, and North America. On the steppes of the Trans-Himalayas and the deserts of the Northwest (both areas presumed to receive more sunshine per year than forested zones and to be comparatively arid with sparse vegetation) are many highly specialized burrowing lizards, primarily gekkonids and agamids, some of which have apparently taken over the ecological role of snakes.

The diversity of turtles is greatest in the Northeast and the Himalayas (19 and 15, respectively), and tends to decrease with distance from these two zones. The centre of origin of the largest family represented in the Indian region, the Bataguridae, is either northeastern India or the Indo-Malayan region, as the high diversity of living species in the regions suggest (see map in Iverson, 1992b).

Factors influencing herpetofaunal species diversity are largely unknown, and may include differences in litter-productivity (Inger, 1980) and annual moisture regime (Duellman, 1978). Historical components, including invasion by extralimital elements and climatic and vegetational changes, also need to be considered. Human activities, which have had particularly devastating effects on the herpetofauna of the south Asian region, should also be considered. Vitt (1987) summarized factors that may affect snake diversity. These include historical (age of geographical area, source of snake fauna), biogeographical (nearness to taxon distribution centre and to areas of flux), abiotic (latitude, elevation, temperature, moisture, habitat structure, climatic stability) and biotic (prey species richness, prey species diversity, prey abundance, potential predators, and habitat productivity).

4.4. AFFINITIES BETWEEN PHYSIOGRAPHIC ZONES

The Coefficients of Community (Cj) for genera show low (Northwest and the Nicobars) to high (Himalayas and Northeastern India) overlap. Cj was calculated inclusive of the eleven widespread genera: excluding these "tramps" would decrease the inter-zonal generic similarity.

TREE DIAGRAM   DISTANCES

```
                0.000
    NORTHWEST ─────────┐
TRANS-HIMALAYAS ───────┤
      HIMALAYAS ─────┐ │
      NORTHEAST ─────┤ │
       SRI LANKA ──┐ │ │
   WESTERN GHATS ──┤ │ │
   EASTERN GHATS ─┐│ │ │
         DECCAN ──┘│ │ │
ANDAMAN ISLANDS ──┐ │ │
NICOBAR ISLANDS ──┘ │ │
```

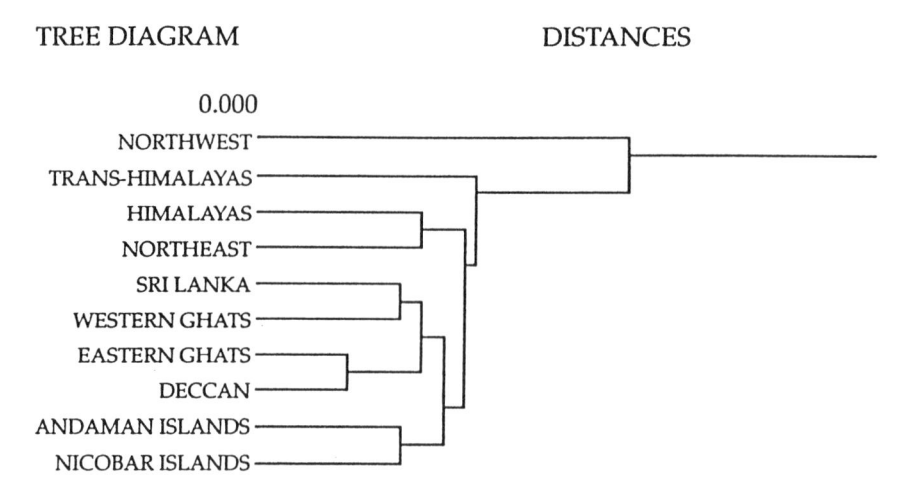

Figure 4. Area cladogram for reptiles, based on Jaccard's Index (generic similarity) between the physiographic zones of south Asia.

Cluster analysis of generic overlap for the 10 physiographic regions within south Asia (Figure 4) reveals the following patterns:

A. The fauna of the Northwest is dissimilar to those of the rest of the physiographic regions in south Asia.

Twenty-six genera are of Palaearctic affinities, including 20 Afro-Mediterranean and 8 Turkomanian-Central Asian genera (Table 5). The extralimital faunal links of the Northwest have been discussed in Section 4.5.

B. The Western Ghats and Sri Lanka are sister areas.

The pattern of biotic association between the Western Ghats and Sri Lanka is in concordance with prevailing theory of invasion of the island by elements from the mainland in successive waves (see Morain, 1984), during its several connections to the mainland, beginning in the Miocene (Cooray, 1967). Erdelen and Preu (1990) hypothesized that during the Quaternary, alternating phases of range expansion of rainforest and contraction of semideciduous and savannah allowed the exchange of rainforest species during the land bridge phases over the Palk Straits.

C. The two Bay Island groups (the Andaman and Nicobars) are sister areas.

It is contended that the reptile fauna of the Andaman and Nicobars is derived from the southeast Asian mainland, the fauna of the first closer to Myanmar, that of the second to the fauna of Thailand (Biswas and Sanyal, 1980). However, these two faunas are closer to each other than either is to the Indian mainland fauna, with many genera and species in common. Endemicity among the reptiles of these islands is also high, accounting for the low overlaps between the faunas. Sixteen of 66 species (24.2%) of reptiles on these islands are unique and not known to occur extralimitally.

    D. The fauna of the Himalayas is closer to that of the Northeast than it is to the Trans-Himalayas.

The Himalayas show an admixture of the fauna of the Northeast and of the Trans-Himalayas, although the elements from the first zone dominate. The genera common to the Northeast and the Himalayas that do not occur in the Trans-Himalayan zone include *Indotestudo*, *Psammodynastes*, and *Trimeresurus*, while the two Himalayan regions share a single genus *(Argyrogena)* exclusively.

    E. Eastern Ghats and the Deccan are sister areas.

At least a major reason for the closeness of the two faunas is that many of the species in common are "weedy" species that are frequently human commensals, or live in the proximity of human dwellings. Presumably human activities in the once forested Eastern Ghats have had devastating effects on the land and its biota. This concordance appears to support Endler's (1982) debatable (see Parenti, 1990) generalization that cladistic concordance may reflect shared environmental effects, not history.

    F. The fauna of the Northeast is not similar to that of the Western Ghats, which is at variance with Hora's (1949) Satpura Hypothesis.

The low faunal overlap between these two regions is due in part to the presence of endemics in both the regions (Northeast two, Western Ghats six). Additionally, 44 genera are common to the Western Ghats and Sri Lanka, which have been considered sister areas, four of which exclusively occur in these two zones. The Northeast shares 2 genera with its sister area, the Himalayas, that do not occur in any other zones. The proportion of genera of reptiles exclusively shared by the Northeast and the Western Ghats, at least within south Asia (2 out of 39, or 5.1%: *Draco* and *Salea*) is lower than for amphibians (5 out of 28, or 17.9%, including *Rhacophorus*, *Pedostibes*, *Micrixalus*, *Philautus*, and *Gegenophis*). In addition, 2 genera, *Trimeresurus* and *Indotestudo*, occur in some of the intervening areas (the northern parts of the Eastern Ghats and the Himalayas). All these taxa are absent in the relatively more xeric intervening zone (the Deccan). The similarity of the fauna of the Western Ghats to that of the Northeast is thus inexplicably less for reptiles than it is for amphibians. This is despite the fact that excessive dry conditions that exist in the intervening Deccan are more likely to stop the dispersal of amphibians than of the reptiles, due to physiological factors.

    The turtle *Geoemyda silvatica* (sometimes assigned to the genus *Heosemys*), distributed in the Western Ghats (Das, 1991), has close relatives in southeast Asia (Moll *et al.*, 1986), and these workers reassigned the species to its original genus (*Geoemyda*). However, Yasukawa *et al.* (1992) have argued that this allocation may be premature, suggesting the retention of the taxon in the genus *Heosemys* until the controversy is resolved satisfactorily. The comparative morphological data on this species and allies in Moll *et al.* (1986), besides the distribution of these turtles, suggest that the Indian species may warrant the creation of a genus to accommodate it.

Biogeographers commonly evoke Hora's (1949) Satpura Hypothesis: the dispersal of the southeast Asian biota to the Western Ghats through the once forested Siwaliks that supposedly acted as a causeway (but see below) to explain the disjunct distribution of several co-occurring taxa from the Western Ghats and northeastern India. Following the Eocene, changes in the flora of the Indian region included the gradual recession of evergreen forests and their replacement by semi-evergreen and eventually, by deciduous and savannah vegetation (van der Hammen, 1983). Peninsular India has experienced considerable climatic and correlated vegetational changes due to anthropogenic reasons over the last millennium too (Randhawa, 1945). This has transformed much of the remnant ancient tropical subhumid and dry deciduous forests into savannas, this change also simulated by farmlands (which account for 50% of the total land area of India) through the cultivation of graminaceous crops (Misra, 1983). Hence, explanations on the dispersal and speciation of the biota of the Indian region, due to lack of data on forest types in the area beyond historic times, will remain open to question.

Hora's hypothesis has been reviewed by numerous authors (*e.g.*, Dilger, 1952; Mani, 1974e; Kottelat, 1989), and it is generally concluded that the Satpura Hypothesis is without geological support (but see Swan, 1993), the disjunct distribution shown by many taxa of plants and animals thought to be remnants of an ancient wider distribution. Mathur (1984) presented evidence of the existence of tropical rainforests as far north as northern India during the late Miocene, prior to 15 m.y.b.p. Alternative hypotheses concerning the discontinuities of ranges of Indian and southeast Asian taxa have been reviewed by Erdelen (1989).

4.5. AFFINITIES WITH EXTRALIMITAL FAUNA

Excluding the 38 endemic genera (Table 4) and 12 genera that are considered Indian radiation (Table 5), the reptile fauna of the south Asian region contains 120 extralimital (or allochthonous) and unknown elements. The extralimital fauna is composed of five complexes: 33 are Palaearctic, including 10 (8.3%) Turkomanian-Central Asian and 23 (19.2%) Afro-Mediterranean genera; 49 are Oriental, including 10 (8.3%) Tibeto-Yunnanese and 42 (35%) Indo-Malayan genera, plus two (1.7%) with other affinities (Table 6). Twenty-three genera (19.2%) are considered transitional, the distribution of member species focussed on bordering regions. The centre of origin of another 10 (8.3%) genera are unknown.

Seventeen and 11 of the 23 (52%) transitional genera occur in the Northeast and Northwest, respectively, suggesting that the physico-climatic barriers of the region are incomplete and may act as a filter. For 3 genera, sister species have been identified outside the Indian region, the Kirthar range being suspected to separate each species pair (Table 7).

As shown by the amphibian fauna (Inger and Dutta, 1986), the regions abutting the continental areas have high faunal influence from extralimital sources. The least mean overlaps in the Coefficients of Community between the faunas of the 10 zones occur in the species from the Bay Islands of the Andamans and Nicobars, and the continental island of Sri Lanka. The reptiles of the Bay Islands have been shown to have closer affinities to the southeast Asian fauna than to the ones on the Indian mainland (Biswas and Sanyal, 1980).

The fauna of the Northwest is largely Palaearctic, that of the Northeast overwhelmingly Oriental. West to east across the northern Indian subcontinent, there is a progressive depletion of Palaearctic fauna, with an apparent compensatory increase in the Oriental fauna (Table 6).

Most of the genera of reptiles on Sri Lanka are shared with India, suggesting their origin either on mainland India or on Sri Lanka and subsequent dispersal over the straits between the two land masses that acted as a bridge during land bridge phases. However, the other members of the genus of the uropeltid *Cylindrophis maculatus* (till recently assigned to a family of their own, the Cylindrophiidae) occur in southeast Asia to which Sri Lanka was never connected. Another squamate, the agamid *Cophotis ceylanica* from Sri Lanka, has a sister species, *C. sumatrana*, on the Indonesian islands of Sumatra and Java (although in his unpublished work, Moody, 1980, assigned the Sundaic species to a different genus, whose affinities lie with other agamid genera, rather than with the Sri Lankan form). These remarkable disjunct distributions may be due to the extinction of sister taxa from the mainland due to climatic changes, as suggested for *Cylindrophis* by Cadle *et al.* (1990). The gecko *Hemiphyllodactylus typus typus* has also been recorded from the Nicobars, and is otherwise widespread in the southeast Asian archipelago (Welch *et al.*, 1990), and its introduction on Sri Lanka and the Bay Islands through human agencies appears likely.

Two enigmatic taxa are *Geochelone elegans* and *Chamaeleo zeylanicus*, which are known from Sri Lanka, the Northwest, the Deccan, Eastern Ghats, and in the case of the first species, also the Western Ghats. Their closest relatives are Sub-Saharan-Madagascan in distribution, although *G. elegans* has a sister species, *G. platynota*, in southwestern Myanmar. The disjunct distribution of these groups may be the result of their extinction in western Asia, possibly a result of desiccation and correlated vegetational changes in Iran, western Pakistan and, in the case of *Geochelone*, the Arabian peninsula and northern Africa. An alternate, and more dramatic, explanation is that these are relicts from the time of India's attachment to the African plate. Other Ethiopian elements present in south Asia, among the recent mammalian fauna, include *Panthera leo* (the lion), *Hyaena hyaena* (striped hyaena), *Mellivora capensis* (ratel or honey badger), as well as many in the prehistoric past, including species related to living hippopotamus, chimpanzee, baboon, aardvark, and giraffe that are today found in Africa (Durand, 1836; Colbert, 1933; Pilgrim, 1937; Mukherjee, 1966; Prater, 1980), some of which show similar disjunct distribution. The sequence of breakup of Gondwanaland, separating the Indian plate from the Afro-Antarctico-Australian one and its union with the Asian land mass has been shown in Smith and Briden (1977).

Darlington (1959) believed that larger areas tend to be the sources of the faunas of adjacent, smaller areas. Yet, the Myanmar-Thailand-Malay Peninsula-Indochina region, which together constitutes a land surface of slightly over two million square kilometres, significantly smaller than the land area of south Asia (*circa* 4.36 million square kilometres), has only 12 genera of reptiles that are clearly Indian radiation, four (including *Calotes sensu stricto*, *Gavialis*, *Kachuga*, and *Lissemys*) of which occur only in the peripheral regions of the Indo-Malayan subrealm. On the other hand, as many as 42 Indo-Malayan genera are represented in the Indian region. The scarcity of a distinctly Indian fauna outside the region and the abundance of clearly allochthonous genera within south Asia, after correcting for land surface area, may at first give the impression that the Indian region acts as an ecological trap (*sensu* Morain, 1984), whereby taxa can invade and subsequently radiate, but cannot emigrate easily.

The land and sea surface area of the entire Sunda region, including all the islands of the Greater and Lesser Sundas (listed by Lawlor, 1986: 121) and the relatively shallow adjacent areas (maximum extent of the land bridges estimated by tracing the 120 m line around extant islands, following Heaney, 1986) of the South China Sea, Java Sea, and the Straits of Malacca, is approximately 2.3 million sq km. The Late Pleistocene was marked with sea-level drops of as much as 120 m below present levels (Bartlett and Barghoorn, 1973; Gascoyne *et al.*, 1979; Bloom, 1983), when island hopping faunas derived in the Sundas could have invaded the mainland, and vice-versa. Even assuming that the Indo-Malayan region, including the entire Sunda Shelf (present islands and the surrounding seas) became available as sources of faunal diversification and subsequent invasion during Pleistocene glaciations, the total area potentially available as extralimital faunal source, *ca.* 4.3 million sq km (see Figure 7A in Lekagul and McNeely, 1988; also Figure 5.5 in Morley and Flenley, 1987, for generalized palaeogeographical reconstruction of the Sunda region during a Quaternary glacial maxima), close to the land area of the south Asian region, still fails to counter the argument that the Indo-Malayan elements are better represented in south Asia than distinctly Indian ones in the Indo-Malayan region, after correcting for land area.

The periodic marine inundation and land bridges in the Sunda archipelago must have created many more opportunities for faunal speciation and subsequent invasion into the adjacent landmass than speciation within south Asia, where, being for the greater part a continuous land mass, evolution may have proceeded at a slower pace. Archipelagos are potentially more favourable environments for "explosive evolution" and diversification compared to a single island or even a continent (the "archipelago effect" of Carlquist, 1965) due to its wider ecological opportunities and barriers between islands. Relatively more stable ecosystems but fewer species must have evolved, according to this line of reasoning, on continental land masses, these tending to be relatively more sedentary than the biota of archipelagos.

Most of the "invading species" from Indo-Malaya appear to use habitats and probably fill niches not utilized by indigenous species, particularly those within rainforests. Indian elements in southeast Asia are largely aquatic (*Kachuga, Lissemys, Melanochelys,* and *Gavialis*) and human commensals or otherwise adaptable to habitats altered through human activities (*Ahaetulla, Calotes* and *Hemidactylus*). In summary, the large proportion of Indo-Malayan elements in south Asia may be the result of greater opportunity of speciation in southeast Asia, especially in the Sundas, which is thought to have produced species that emigrated into the mainland during land bridge stages. On the other hand, the relatively few distinctly Indian taxa in the Indo-Malayan region may be due to the slower rates of evolution on peninsular India of a largely nonemigrating type of fauna.

4.6. BARRIERS AND SPECIATION

Speciation typically works through populations passing through gradual stages of differentiation, from localized deme to race and subspecies, finally to distinct species (White, 1981). Better distributional data on the taxa from the Indian region will allow a more refined biogeographic analysis, as well as help understand speciation mechanisms. In this section, I analyze speciation mechanisms thought to be in operation based on the available information on the distribution and ecology of reptile sister species.

The physiographic zones and their presumed barriers have been shown in Figure 1. Some of the geographic barriers, such as rivers (*e.g.*, the Ganga) and low mountain ranges (*e.g.*, the eastern and western outliers of the Himalayas) function as filters (*sensu* Simpson, 1962), impeding movement and stopping the ranges of some but not all taxa. High mountain ranges such as the Himalayas act as "sweepstakes", formidable enough to virtually stop faunal invasions.

Das and Pritchard (1990) showed that the hill ranges of the Western Ghats, in southwestern India, act as an incomplete barrier to the ranges of *Melanochelys trijuga trijuga* (to the east) and *M. trijuga coronata* (to the west), with intergradient populations occurring on the ridges. The dispersal model of speciation (Mayr, 1962; 76), which postulates that the colonizing propagules from the parent population evolve along different paths, is suspected to be in operation in this case. Given time, these two subspecies may evolve into distinct species, but for the moment, a subspecific allocation is more appropriate, as the intergradient population suggests. An alternative explanation involving the vicariant separation of previously widespread taxa cannot, however, be ruled out. Within this scenario, the orogeny of the Western Ghats broke up the once continuous range of a widespread species, ultimately leading to the evolution of distinct subspecies to the east and west of the range. Intensive fieldwork to discover populations on the lowlands west of the northern sections of the Western Ghats may provide information on the mode of differentiation of these turtles.

The rainforest species, especially the so-called "relict species" (see de Silva, 1990; Nanayakkara, 1991) of Sri Lanka, such as uropeltid snakes and lizards of the genera *Otocryptis* and *Calodactylodes*, are restricted to the mesic forest zone of southwestern Sri Lanka, their closest relatives, sister species, and in some cases, vicars, known from southwestern India (Western Ghats). It appears that the intervening savannah type of vegetation in northern Sri Lanka and on the southeastern tip of peninsular India is a more important barrier than the shallow saltwater stretch separating the two physiographic zones. Support for this lies in the presence on northern Sri Lanka of many widely distributed reptile species from the Indian peninsula that have managed to cross the saltwater gap to arrive in Sri Lanka or vice versa. The presumed emigrants are associated with xeric conditions, and include the arboreal *Calotes versicolor*, *Chamaeleo zeylanicus*, *Hemidactylus scabriceps*, and *H. maculatus* and the terrestrial *Geochelone elegans* and *Mabuya bibroni*. Erdelen and Preu's (1990) model of alternating phases of mesic (rainforest) and xeric (dry deciduous and savannah-type) vegetation across the straits at various times during the Quaternary may explain how both the mesic and xeric components of the island's reptile fauna may have managed to invade the island from the mainland colonization source, or vice versa, without physically crossing the saltwater stretch. On the other hand, the evolution of distinct Sri Lankan taxa that are endemic (*e.g.*, *Aspidura, Pseudotyphlops,* and *Ceratophora*) and the presence of southeast Asian elements (including *Cophotis* and *Cylindrophis*) on Sri Lanka may be linked to the existence of aseasonal rainforests, similar to those in the Indo-Malayan region, rather than the distinctly seasonal ones in southwestern India.

More than one barrier may lie between the ranges of two sister species, as between *Cylindrophis maculatus* and *C. ruffus* (Table 7). Sharp climatic and vegetational differences in adjacent land mass and intervening plains accounted for 11 (36.7%) of the 30 barriers among 26 sister species. Of these, land surfaces with marked climatic and/or floristic differences (Deccan-Western Ghats, northern and southeastern Sri Lanka and northwestern highlands of Pakistan-Indus Valley) were found correlated with 10 (33.3%) of the species breaks, while intervening plains (north of the Godavari) lie between the ranges of one (3.3%) sister species. Saltwater stretches (including the Palk Straits and the Great Channel, which separates the Nicobars from Sumatra and its satellite islands) lie between five (19.2%) of species-pairs. Other barriers include hill ranges (the Naga-Arakan-Mishmi, Kirthar and the northwestern highlands of Pakistan) with 12 (46.2%) cases and large rivers (Ganga and Brahmaputra) with two (7.7%) representatives.

Fourteen of the 26 reptile species-pairs (or 53.9%) are forest species, the rest (46.1%) associated with various nonforest habitats, including freshwater bodies, scrub land and deserts. Forest and nonforest species contribute unequally to cases supporting the dispersal model (5 and 9, respectively), while forest species were much more commonly represented in the vicariance model than were the nonforest ones (nine and one, respectively).

Of the three speciation modes believed to be in operation in 26 sister species' cases (Table 7), the vicariance mode is considered responsible for 10 (38.46%) of the cases, and is associated with sharp climatic/topographical barriers (Deccan and the plains of northern Sri Lanka), mountain ranges (Naga-Arakan-Mishmi Hills), as well as shallow continental saltwater stretches (Palk Straits). Dispersal accounted for as many as 14 (53.9%), and is shown by sister species separated by hill ranges (the Naga-Arakan and Kirthar), plains (area north of the Godavari), rivers (Ganga) and oceanic saltwater stretches (the 10° Channel and the Great Channel). The refugial mode appears the rarest, with two cases (7.7%), the barriers to the species-pairs being a mountain (Western Ghats) and a sharp mesic-xeric gradient (flood plains of Ganga-northeastern peninsular India). The Naga-Arakan ranges, which form the eastern/southeastern boundary of the Indian region (Figure 1), appear a major barrier, but invasions appear to have taken place both along the coast (*Lissemys punctata - L. scutata;* dispersal probably along the Arakan coast) and over the forested ridges (*Stoliczkaia khasiensis - S. borneensis*).

Overall, the sequential proportion of speciation modes is similar in both birds (data from Ripley and Beehler, 1990) and reptiles (Table 7)—dispersal 50% and 53.9%, vicariance 22% and 38.5%, and refugial 16% and 7.7%, for birds and reptile species-pairs, respectively. A fourth speciation mode, parapatric (12% of cases) was observed in birds, but not in reptiles.

Mountain ranges intervene between the ranges of reptile species-pairs much more frequently (40% of the barriers) than in birds (20%). However, despite being better equipped to invade new areas by flight, birds are apparently stopped more often by water barriers, including rivers (36.4% of the barriers) and saltwater passages (27.3%) than are reptiles (6.6% and 16.7%, respectively), for whom rafting and swimming must be the only possible modes of dispersal across water barriers, although lowered sea levels have certainly allowed the invasion of many taxa across saltwater stretches in the Indian region as well as in the southeast Asian archipelago. Lack's (1976) assertion that isolation is of little consequence as a barrier to the dispersal of birds has been shown to be without support by Reed (1987), who found a significant inverse correlation between the degree of isolation from the mainland colonization source and the numbers of breeding birds on islands. The probable reason for the presence of relatively fewer water barriers between the reptiles species-pairs isolated on southwestern India, and across the shallow saltwater stretch of the Palk, on Sri Lanka, than birds is that species involved are primarily forest dwellers. Thus they were likely to be either residents at the time of Sri Lanka's first detachment from the tip of the Indian peninsula or invaded the island from the mainland, or the mainland from the island during the Quaternary, when the lowering of sea levels allowed the extension and contraction of tropical forests, according to Erdelen and Preu's (1989) model.

Plains-mountains discontinuity stopped 40% of the reptile species-pairs, but only 20% of the birds. A generalization to be drawn from this observation is that reptiles are more closely linked to particular habitat types than birds, being relatively more sedentary.

In conclusion, both the dispersal and vicariance models are considered important in the speciation of reptiles in south Asia. The refugial speciation model is rare. The dispersal model is supported by more active nonforest species than presumably sedentary forest species; the vicariance model primarily by forest species.

4.7. DISJUNCT DISTRIBUTION OF TAXA

Marked discontinuity in the distribution of several species in the subcontinent appears remarkable, even after allowing for unequal collecting effort and the often poorly known phylogenetic relationships. These include

Chrysopelea ornata, which has populations in the Western Ghats and the Northeast. Less dramatic range discontinuities are also known: the map of the known localities of *Bungarus sindanus* in Khan (1985b: Fig. 1) shows three clearly allopatric populations, each currently considered subspecifically distinct (Khan, 1985b; Welch, 1988).

Disjunct distributions at the generic level are shown both by the amphibian and reptile fauna of the region. Species belonging to three genera, *Ansonia* (*fide* Inger, 1960) an amphibian, and *Cnemaspis* (Welch *et al.*, 1990) and *Dasia* (*fide* Inger and Brown, 1980), both reptiles, that occur in the Western Ghats have close relatives in southeast Asia. Their absence in the Northeast may be due to the region's markedly seasonal climate, including cold winters. Several genera, as already discussed, are distributed in the Western Ghats and, then after a gap of several hundred kilometres, reappear again in the Northeast, including the amphibian genera *Philautus*, the bush frogs and *Nectophryne*, the tree toads (see Jayaram, 1974).

An example of marked discontinuity in distribution along apparently homogenous land mass is shown by the testudinid *Geochelone elegans*, with populations focused on northwestern India and eastern Pakistan, southeastern India and Sri Lanka (Das, 1991; Iverson, 1992a). It is likely that these populations will eventually be recognised as three separate subspecies (John Frazier, *pers. comm.*, 1990). Proponents of ESC would claim a species rank for all these isolated, clearly allopatric and diagnosable populations. Thus, with further study, many of such isolated populations may be elevated to species rank, increasing the total number of species in south Asia.

Chapter 5

TABLES

TABLE 1
CHECKLIST OF REPTILES OF SOUTH ASIA

* = believed to be locally extinct
** = taxa from politically disputed region
*** = type locality in original description not precise

CROCODILIA

CROCODYLIDAE

1. *Crocodylus palustris* Lesson, 1831: Bangladesh*, India, Nepal, Pakistan, Sri Lanka
2. *Crocodylus porosus* Schneider, 1801: Bangladesh, India, Sri Lanka

GAVIALIIDAE

3. *Gavialis gangeticus* (Gmelin, 1789): Bangladesh, Bhutan*, India, Nepal, Pakistan

TESTUDINES

DERMOCHELYIDAE

4. *Dermochelys coriacea* (Vandelli, 1761): Bangladesh, India, Pakistan, Sri Lanka

CHELONIIDAE

5. *Caretta caretta* (Linnaeus, 1758): Bangladesh, India, Maldives, Pakistan, Sri Lanka
6. *Chelonia mydas* (Linnaeus, 1758): Bangladesh, India, Maldives, Pakistan, Sri Lanka
7. *Eretmochelys imbricata* (Linnaeus, 1766): Bangladesh, India, Maldives, Sri Lanka

8. *Lepidochelys olivacea* (Eschscholtz, 1829): Bangladesh, India, Maldives, Pakistan, Sri Lanka

BATAGURIDAE

9. *Batagur baska* (Gray, 1831)
   Batagur baska baska (Gray, 1831): Bangladesh, India
10. *Cuora amboinensis* (Daudin, 1801)
    Cuora amboinensis kamaroma Rummler & Fritz, 1991: Bangladesh, India
11. *Cyclemys dentata* (Gray, 1831): Bangladesh, India
12. *Geoclemys hamiltonii* (Gray, 1831): Bangladesh, India, Pakistan
13. *Geoemyda silvatica* Henderson, 1912: India
14. *Hardella thurjii* (Gray, 1831)
    Hardella thurjii thurjii (Gray, 1831): Bangladesh, India, Nepal
    Hardella thurjii indi (Gray, 1870): Pakistan
15. *Kachuga dhongoka* (Gray, 1834): Bangladesh, India, Nepal
16. *Kachuga kachuga* (Gray, 1831): Bangladesh, India, Nepal
17. *Kachuga smithii* (Gray, 1863)
    Kachuga smithii smithii (Gray, 1863): Bangladesh, India, Pakistan
    Kachuga smithii pallidipes Moll, 1987: India, Nepal
18. *Kachuga sylhetensis* (Jerdon, 1870): Bangladesh, India
19. *Kachuga tecta* (Gray, 1831): Bangladesh, India, Nepal, Pakistan
20. *Kachuga tentoria* (Gray, 1834)
    Kachuga tentoria tentoria (Gray, 1834): India
    Kachuga tentoria circumdata (Mertens, 1969): India
    Kachuga tentoria flaviventer (Günther, 1864): Bangladesh, India
21. *Melanochelys tricarinata* (Blyth, 1856): Bangladesh, India, Nepal
22. *Melanochelys trijuga* (Schweigger, 1812)
    Melanochelys trijuga trijuga (Schweigger, 1812): India
    Melanochelys trijuga coronata (Anderson, 1879): India
    Melanochelys trijuga indopeninsularis (Annandale, 1913): Bangladesh, India, Nepal
    Melanochelys trijuga parkeri (Deraniyagala, 1939): Sri Lanka
    Melanochelys trijuga thermalis (Lesson, 1830): India, Maldives, Sri Lanka
23. *Morenia petersi* (Anderson, 1879): Bangladesh, India
24. *Pyxidea mouhotii* (Gray, 1862): India

TESTUDINIDAE

    25. *Geochelone elegans* (Schoepff, 1795): India, Pakistan, Sri Lanka

    26. *Indotestudo elongata* (Blyth, 1853): Bangladesh, India, Nepal

    27. *Indotestudo forstenii* (Schlegel & Müller, 1844): India

    28. *Manouria emys* (Schlegel & Müller, 1840)
        Manouria emys phayrei (Blyth, 1853): Bangladesh, India

    29. *Testudo horsfieldii* Gray, 1844
        Testudo horsfieldii horsfieldii Gray, 1844: Pakistan

TRIONYCHIDAE

    30. *Aspideretes gangeticus* (Cuvier, 1825): Bangladesh, India, Nepal, Pakistan

    31. *Aspideretes hurum* (Gray, 1831): Bangladesh, India

    32. *Aspideretes leithii* (Gray, 1872): India

    33. *Aspideretes nigricans* (Anderson, 1875): Bangladesh

    34. *Chitra indica* (Gray, 1831): Bangladesh, India, Nepal, Pakistan

    35. *Lissemys punctata* (Lacépède, 1788)
        Lissemys punctata punctata (Lacépède, 1788): India, Sri Lanka
        Lissemys punctata andersoni Webb, 1980: Bangladesh, India, Nepal, Pakistan

    36. *Pelochelys bibroni* (Owen, 1853): Bangladesh, India

SAURIA

GEKKONIDAE

    37. *Agamura femoralis* (Smith, 1933): Pakistan

    38. *Agamura misonnei* (Whitte, 1973): Pakistan

    39. *Agamura persica* (Duméril, 1856): Pakistan

    40. *Alsophylax boehmi* (Szczerbak, 1991): India/Pakistan**

    41. *Asiocolotes depressus* (Minton & Anderson, 1965): Pakistan

    42. *Bunopus tuberculatus* (Blanford, 1874): Pakistan

    43. *Calodactylodes aureus* (Beddome, 1870): India

    44. *Calodactylodes illingworthi* (Deraniyagala, 1953): Sri Lanka

    45. *Cnemaspis beddomei* (Theobald, 1876): India

    46. *Cnemaspis boiei* (Gray, 1842): India***

47. *Cnemaspis goaensis* (Sharma, 1976): India
48. *Cnemaspis indica* (Gray, 1846): India
49. *Cnemaspis jerdoni* (Theobald, 1868)
    Cnemaspis jerdoni jerdoni (Theobald, 1868): India
    Cnemaspis jerdoni scalpensis (Ferguson, 1877): Sri Lanka
50. *Cnemaspis kandianus* (Kelaart, 1852): India, Sri Lanka
51. *Cnemaspis littoralis* (Jerdon, 1853): India
52. *Cnemaspis mysoriensis* (Jerdon, 1853): India
53. *Cnemaspis nairi* Inger, Marx & Koshy, 1984: India
54. *Cnemaspis ornatus* (Beddome, 1870): India
55. *Cnemaspis podihuna* Deraniyagala, 1944: Sri Lanka
56. *Cnemaspis sisparensis* (Theobald, 1876): India
57. *Cnemaspis tropidogaster* (Boulenger, 1885): India, Sri Lanka
58. *Cnemaspis wynadensis* (Beddome, 1870): India
59. *Cosymbotus platyurus* (Schneider, 1792): Bhutan, India, Nepal, Sri Lanka
60. *Crossobamon eversmanni* (Wiegmann, 1834)
    Crossobamon eversmanni eversmanni (Wiegmann, 1834): Pakistan
    Crossobamon eversmanni maynardi (Smith, 1933): Pakistan
61. *Crossobamon orientalis* (Blanford, 1876): Pakistan
62. *Cyrtopodion agamuroides* Nikolskii, 1900: Pakistan
63. *Cyrtopodion fedtschenkoi* (Strauch, 1887): Pakistan
64. *Cyrtopodion kachhensis* (Stoliczka, 1872): India, Pakistan
65. *Cyrtopodion scaber* (Heyden in Rüppell, 1827): India, Pakistan
66. *Cyrtopodion watsoni* (Murray, 1892): Pakistan
67. *Eublepharis hardwickii* Gray, 1827: Bangladesh, India
68. *Eublepharis macularius* (Blyth, 1854): India, Pakistan
69. *Geckoella collegalensis* (Beddome, 1870): India, Sri Lanka
70. *Geckoella dekkanensis* (Günther, 1864): India
71. *Geckoella jeyporensis* (Beddome, 1877): India
72. *Geckoella nebulosa* (Beddome, 1870): India
73. *Geckoella triedrus* (Günther, 1864): Sri Lanka
74. *Geckoella yakhuna* (Deraniyagala, 1945): Sri Lanka
75. *Gehyra mutilata* (Wiegmann, 1834): India, Sri Lanka

76. *Gekko gecko* (Linnaeus, 1758)
    Gekko gecko gecko (Linnaeus, 1758): India, Nepal, Pakistan
    Gekko gecko azhari Mertens, 1955: Bangladesh
77. *Gekko smithii* Gray, 1842: India
78. *Gekko verreauxi* (Tytler, 1864): India
79. *Gonydactylus chitralensis* (Smith, 1935): Pakistan
80. *Gonydactylus dattanensis* (Khan, 1980): Pakistan
81. *Gonydactylus fasciolatus* (Blyth, 1860): India
82. *Gonydactylus frenatus* (Günther, 1864): Sri Lanka
83. *Gonydactylus gubernatoris* (Annandale, 1913): India
84. *Gonydactylus himalayanus* (Duda & Sahi, 1978): India, Nepal
85. *Gonydactylus khasiensis* (Jerdon, 1870)
    Gonydactylus khasiensis khasiensis (Jerdon, 1870): India
86. *Gonydactylus lawderanus* (Stoliczka, 1871): India
87. *Gonydactylus malcolmsmithi* (Constable, 1949): India
88. *Gonydactylus mansarulus* (Duda & Sahi, 1978): India
89. *Gonydactylus mintoni* (Szczerbak & Golubev, 1981): Pakistan
90. *Gonydactylus pulchellus* (Gray, 1828): India
91. *Gonydactylus rubidus* (Blyth, 1860): India
92. *Gonydactylus stoliczkai* (Steindachner, 1869): India, Pakistan
93. *Gonydactylus walli* (Ingoldby, 1922): India/Pakistan**
94. *Hemidactylus anamallensis* (Günther, 1875): India
95. *Hemidactylus bowringii* (Gray, 1845): Bangladesh, India
96. *Hemidactylus brookii* (Gray, 1845): Bangladesh, Bhutan, India, Maldives, Nepal, Pakistan, Sri Lanka
97. *Hemidactylus depressus* Gray, 1842: Sri Lanka
98. *Hemidactylus flaviviridis* Rüppell, 1840: Bangladesh, India, Nepal, Pakistan
99. *Hemidactylus frenatus* Duméril & Bibron, 1836: Bangladesh, Bhutan, India, Maldives, Nepal, Pakistan, Sri Lanka
100. *Hemidactylus garnotii* Duméril & Bibron, 1836: Bhutan, India
101. *Hemidactylus giganteus* Stoliczka, 1871: India
102. *Hemidactylus gracilis* Blanford, 1870: India
103. *Hemidactylus karenorum* (Theobald, 1868): India
104. *Hemidactylus leschenaulti* Duméril & Bibron, 1836: India, Pakistan, Sri Lanka

105. *Hemidactylus maculatus* Duméril & Bibron, 1836
    Hemidactylus maculatus maculatus Duméril & Bibron, 1836: India
    Hemidactylus maculatus hunae Deraniyagala, 1937: India, Sri Lanka
106. *Hemidactylus mahendrai* Shukla, 1983: India
107. *Hemidactylus persicus* Anderson, 1872: Pakistan
108. *Hemidactylus porbandarensis* Sharma, 1981: India
109. *Hemidactylus prashadi* Smith, 1935: India
110. *Hemidactylus reticulatus* Beddome, 1870: India
111. *Hemidactylus scabriceps* (Annandale, 1906): India, Sri Lanka
112. *Hemidactylus subtriedrus* Jerdon, 1853: India
113. *Hemidactylus triedrus* (Daudin, 1802)
    Hemidactys triedrus triedrus (Daudin, 1802): India, Pakistan
    Hemidactylus triedrus lankae Deraniyagala, 1953: Sri Lanka
114. *Hemidactylus turcicus* (Linnaeus, 1758)
    Hemidactylus turcicus turcicus (Linnaeus, 1758): Pakistan
115. *Hemiphyllodactylus typus* Bleeker, 1860
    Hemiphyllodactylus typus typus Bleeker, 1860: India, Sri Lanka
    Hemiphyllodactylus typus aurantiacus Beddome, 1870: India
116. *Lepidodactylus lugubris* (Duméril & Bibron, 1836): India, Sri Lanka
117. *Microgecko helenae* Nikolsky, 1907: Pakistan
118. *Phelsuma andamanense* Blyth, 1860: India
119. *Pristurus rupestris* Blanford, 1874: Pakistan
120. *Ptychozoon kuhli* Stejneger, 1902: India
121. *Ptyodactylus homolepis* Blanford, 1876: Pakistan
122. *Tenuidactylus battalensis* Khan, 1993: Pakistan
123. *Tenuidactylus baturensis* Khan, 1992: Pakistan
124. *Tenuidactylus fortmunroi* Khan, 1993: Pakistan
125. *Tenuidactylus indusoani* (Khan, 1988): Pakistan
126. *Tenuidactylus kohsulaimanai* Khan, 1991: Pakistan
127. *Tenuidactylus montiumsalsorum* (Annandale, 1913): Pakistan
128. *Tenuidactylus rohtasfortai* Khan & Tasnim, 1990: Pakistan
129. *Teratolepis albofasciatus* (Grandison & Soman, 1963): India
130. *Teratolepis fasciata* (Blyth, 1853): Pakistan

131. *Teratoscincus microlepis* Nikolsky, 1899: Pakistan
132. *Teratoscincus scincus* (Schlegel, 1858)
   Teratoscincus scincus keyserlingii (Strauch, 1863): Pakistan
133. *Tropiocolotes persicus* (Nikolsky, 1903)
   Tropiocolotes persicus persicus (Nikolski, 1903): Pakistan
   Tropiocolotes persicus euphorbiacola Minton, Anderson & Anderson, 1970: Pakistan

AGAMIDAE

134. *Bronchocela cristatella* (Kuhl, 1820): India
135. *Bronchocela danieli* Tiwari & Biswas, 1973: India
136. *Bronchocela jubata* Duméril & Bibron, 1837: India
137. *Bufoniceps laungwalensis* (Sharma, 1978): India
138. *Calotes andamanensis* Boulenger, 1891: India
139. *Calotes bhutanensis* (Biswas, 1975): Bhutan
140. *Calotes calotes* (Linnaeus, 1758): India, Sri Lanka
141. *Calotes ceylonensis* (Müller, 1887): Sri Lanka
142. *Calotes ellioti* Günther, 1864
   Calotes ellioti ellioti Günther, 1864: India
   Calotes ellioti amarambalamensis Murthy, 1978: India
143. *Calotes emma* Gray, 1845
   Calotes emma alticristatus (Schmidt, 1927): India
144. *Calotes grandisquamis* Günther, 1875: India
145. *Calotes jerdoni* Günther, "1870," 1871: Bangladesh, India
146. *Calotes liocephalus* Günther, 1872: Sri Lanka
147. *Calotes liolepis* Boulenger, 1885: Sri Lanka
148. *Calotes maria* Gray, 1845: India
149. *Calotes mystaceus* Duméril & Bibron, 1837: India
150. *Calotes nemoricola* Jerdon, 1853: India
151. *Calotes nigrilabris* Peters, 1860: Sri Lanka
152. *Calotes rouxii* Duméril & Bibron, 1837: India
153. *Calotes versicolor* (Daudin, 1802)
   Calotes versicolor versicolor (Daudin, 1802): Bangladesh, Bhutan, India, Maldives, Nepal, Pakistan, Sri Lanka
   Calotes versicolor nigrigularis Auffenberg & Rehman, 1993: India, Pakistan

154. *Ceratophora aspera* Günther, 1864: Sri Lanka
155. *Ceratophora stoddartii* Gray, 1834: Sri Lanka
156. *Ceratophora tennentii* Günther, 1861: Sri Lanka
157. *Cophotis ceylanica* Peters, 1861: Sri Lanka
158. *Coryphophylax subcristatus* (Blyth, 1860): India
159. *Draco blanfordii* Boulenger, 1885
    Draco blanfordii norvillii (Alcock, 1895): Bangladesh, India
160. *Draco dussumieri* Duméril & Bibron, 1837: India
161. *Japalura andersoniana* Annandale, 1905: Bhutan, India
162. *Japalura kumaonensis* (Annandale, 1907): India, Nepal
163. *Japalura major* (Jerdon, 1870): India, Nepal
164. *Japalura planidorsata* Jerdon, 1870: India
165. *Japalura tricarinatus* (Blyth, 1854): India, Nepal
166. *Japalura variegata* Gray, 1853: Bhutan, India, Nepal
167. *Laudakia agrorensis* (Stoliczka, 1872): India, Pakistan
168. *Laudakia caucasicus* (Eichwald, 1831): Pakistan
169. *Laudakia himalayanus* (Steindachner, 1867): India, Pakistan
170. *Laudakia melanura* (Blyth, 1854): India, Pakistan
171. *Laudakia minor* (Hardwicke & Gray, 1827): India, Pakistan
172. *Laudakia nupta* (De Filippi, 1843)
    Laudakia nupta nupta (De Filippi, 1843): Pakistan
    Laudakia nupta fusca (Blanford, 1876): Pakistan
173. *Laudakia pakistanica* (Baig, 1989): India/Pakistan**
174. *Laudakia tuberculata* (Hardwicke & Gray, 1827): India, Nepal, Pakistan
175. *Lyriocephalus scutatus* (Linnaeus, 1758): Sri Lanka
176. *Mictopholis austeniana* (Annandale, 1908): India
177. *Oriocalotes paulus* Smith, 1935: India
178. *Otocryptis beddomii* Boulenger, 1885: India
179. *Otocryptis wiegmanni* Wagler, 1830: Sri Lanka
180. *Phrynocephalus alticola* Peters, 1984: India
181. *Phrynocephalus clarkorum* Anderson & Leviton, 1967: Pakistan
182. *Phrynocephalus euptilopus* Alcock & Finn, 1896: Pakistan
183. *Phrynocephalus luteoguttatus* Boulenger, 1887: Pakistan
184. *Phrynocephalus maculatus* Anderson, 1872: Pakistan

185. *Phrynocephalus ornatus* Boulenger, 1887: Pakistan
186. *Phrynocephalus scutellata* (Olivier, 1807): Pakistan
187. *Phrynocephalus theobaldi* Blyth, 1863: India, Nepal
188. *Psammophilus blanfordanus* (Stoliczka, 1870): India
189. *Psammophilus dorsalis* (Gray, 1831): India
190. *Pseudocalotes microlepis* (Boulenger, 1887): India
191. *Ptyctolaemus gularis* (Peters, 1864): India
192. *Salea anamallayana* (Beddome, 1878): India
193. *Salea horsfieldii* Gray, 1845: India
194. *Salea kakhiensis* (Anderson, 1878): India
195. *Sitana ponticeriana* Cuvier, 1844: India, Nepal, Pakistan, Sri Lanka
196. *Trapelus agilis* (Olivier, 1804): India, Pakistan
197. *Trapelus megalonyx* Günther, 1864: Pakistan
198. *Trapelus ruderatus* (Olivier, 1804)
   Trapelus ruderatus baluchiana Smith, 1935: Pakistan
199. *Trapelus rubrigularis* Blanford, 1875: Pakistan
200. *Uromastyx asmussii* (Strauch, 1863): Pakistan
201. *Uromastyx hardwickii* Gray, 1827: India, Pakistan

CHAMAELEONIDAE

202. *Chamaeleo zeylanicus* Laurenti, 1768: India, Pakistan, Sri Lanka

DIBAMIDAE

203. *Dibamus leucurus* (Bleeker, 1860): India

SCINCIDAE

204. *Ablepharus grayanus* (Stoliczka, 1872): India, Pakistan
205. *Ablepharus pannonicus* Fitzinger in Lichtenstein in Eversmann, 1823: India, Pakistan
206. *Barkudia insularis* Annandale, 1917: India
207. *Chalcides ocellatus* (Forsskål, 1775): Pakistan
208. *Chalcides pentadactylus* (Beddome, 1870): India
209. *Chalcidoseps thwaitesii* (Günther, 1872): Sri Lanka
210. *Dasamia rugifera* (Stoliczka, 1870): India

211. *Dasia halianus* (Haly & Nevill, 1887): India, Sri Lanka
212. *Dasia nicobarensis* Biswas & Sanyal, 1977: India
213. *Dasia olivacea* Gray, 1838: India
214. *Dasia subcaeruleum* (Boulenger, 1891): India
215. *Eumeces blythianus* (Anderson, 1871): India
216. *Eumeces poonaensis* Sharma, 1970: India
217. *Eumeces schneideri* (Daudin, 1802)
    Eumeces schneideri schneideri (Daudin, 1802): India
    Eumeces schneideri blythianus (Anderson, 1871): India, Pakistan
    Eumeces schneiderii zarudnyi (Nikolski, 1899): Pakistan
218. *Eumeces taeniolatus* (Blyth, 1854): India, Pakistan
219. *Lankascincus deignani* (Taylor, 1950): Sri Lanka
220. *Lankascincus deraniyagalae* Greer, 1991: Sri Lanka
221. *Lankascincus fallax* (Peters, 1860): Sri Lanka
222. *Lankascincus gansi* Greer, 1991: Sri Lanka
223. *Lankascincus taprobanensis* (Kelaart, 1852): Sri Lanka
224. *Lankascincus taylori* Greer, 1991: Sri Lanka
225. *Lipinia macrotympanum* (Stoliczka, 1873): India
226. *Lipinia quadrivittatum* (Peters, 1867): India
227. *Lygosoma albopunctata* (Gray, 1846): Bangladesh, India, Maldives
228. *Lygosoma ashwamedhi* (Sharma, 1969): India
229. *Lygosoma bowringii* (Günther, 1864): India
230. *Lygosoma goaensis* (Sharma, 1976): India
231. *Lygosoma guentheri* (Peters, 1879): India
232. *Lygosoma lineata* (Gray, 1839): India
233. *Lygosoma pruthi* (Sharma, 1977): India
234. *Lygosoma punctatus* (Gmelin, 1799): Bangladesh, India, Pakistan, Sri Lanka
235. *Lygosoma singha* (Taylor, 1950): Sri Lanka
236. *Lygosoma vosmaeri* (Gray, 1839): Bangladesh, India
237. *Mabuya allapallensis* Schmidt, 1926: India
238. *Mabuya andamanensis* Smith, 1935: India
239. *Mabuya aurata* (Linnaeus, 1758): Pakistan
240. *Mabuya beddomii* (Jerdon, 1870): India, Sri Lanka

241. *Mabuya bibronii* (Gray, 1838): India, Sri Lanka
242. *Mabuya carinata* (Schneider, 1801)
    Mabuya carinata carinata (Schneider, 1801): Bangladesh, India, Maldives, Nepal
    Mabuya carinata lankae Deraniyagala, 1953: Sri Lanka
243. *Mabuya clivicola* Inger, Shaffer, Koshy & Bakde, 1984: India
244. *Mabuya dissimilis* (Hallowell, 1857): Bangladesh, India, Nepal, Pakistan
245. *Mabuya floweri* Taylor, 1950: Sri Lanka
246. *Mabuya gansi* Das, 1991: India
247. *Mabuya innotatus* (Blanfordi, 1870): India
248. *Mabuya macularius* (Blyth, 1853)
    Mabuya macularius macularius (Blyth, 1853): Bangladesh, India, Nepal, Pakistan, Sri Lanka
249. *Mabuya madaraszi* Méhely, 1897: Sri Lanka
250. *Mabuya multifasciata* (Kuhl, 1820): India
251. *Mabuya nagarjuni* Sharma, 1969: India
252. *Mabuya quadratilobus* Bauer & Günther, 1992: Bhutan
253. *Mabuya quadricarinata* Boulenger, 1887: India
254. *Mabuya rudis* Boulenger, 1887: India
255. *Mabuya trivittata* (Hardwicke & Gray, 1827): India
256. *Mabuya tytleri* (Theobald, 1868): India
257. *Nessia bipes* Smith, 1935: Sri Lanka
258. *Nessia burtonii* Gray, 1839: Sri Lanka
259. *Nessia deraniyagalai* Taylor, 1950: Sri Lanka
260. *Nessia didactylus* (Deraniyagala, 1934): Sri Lanka
261. *Nessia hickanala* Deraniyagala, 1940: Sri Lanka
262. *Nessia layardi* (Kelaart, 1853): Sri Lanka
263. *Nessia monodactylus* (Gray, 1839): Sri Lanka
264. *Nessia sarasinorum* (Müller, 1889): Sri Lanka
265. *Ophiomorus blanfordii* Boulenger, 1887: Pakistan
266. *Ophiomorus raithmai* Anderson & Leviton, 1966: India, Pakistan
267. *Ophiomorus tridactylus* (Blyth, 1855): India, Pakistan
268. *Ristella beddomii* Boulenger, 1887: India

269. *Ristella guentheri* Boulenger, 1887: India
270. *Ristella rurkii* Gray, 1839: India
271. *Ristella travancoricus* (Beddome, 1870): India
272. *Scincella bilineatum* (Gray, 1846): India
273. *Scincella capitanea* (Ouboter, 1986): Nepal
274. *Scincella ladacensis* (Günther, 1864)
    Scincella ladacensis ladacensis (Günther, 1864): India, Nepal
    Scincella ladacensis himalayanus (Günther, 1864): India, Nepal, Pakistan
    Scincella ladacensis traghulense (Alcock, 1898): India
275. *Scincella macrotis* (Steindachneri, 1869): India
276. *Scincella sikimmensis* (Blyth, 1853): Bangladesh, Bhutan, India, Nepal
277. *Scincella travancoricum* (Beddome, 1870): India
278. *Scincus mitranus* Anderson, 1871: Pakistan
279. *Sepsophis punctatus* Beddome, 1870: India
280. *Sphenomorphus courcyanus* (Annandale, 1912): India
281. *Sphenomorphus deignani* Taylor, 1950: Sri Lanka
282. *Sphenomorphus dorsicatenatus* Deraniyagala, 1953: Sri Lanka
283. *Sphenomorphus dussumieri* (Duméril & Bibron, 1839): India, Sri Lanka
284. *Sphenomorphus indicus* (Gray, 1853): Bhutan, India
285. *Sphenomorphus maculatus* (Blyth, 1853): Bangladesh, Bhutan, India
286. *Sphenomorphus megalops* (Annandale, 1906): Sri Lanka
287. *Sphenomorphus reevesi* (Gray, 1838)
    Sphenomorphus reevesi reevesi (Gray, 1838): India
288. *Sphenomorphus rufogulus* Taylor, 1950: Sri Lanka
289. *Tropidophorus assamensis* Annandale, 1912: Bangladesh

LACERTIDAE

290. *Acanthodactylus blanfordii* Boulenger, 1918: India, Pakistan
291. *Acanthodactylus cantoris* Günther, 1864: India, Pakistan
292. *Acanthodactylus micropholis* Blanford, 1874: Pakistan
293. *Eremias brevirostris* Stoliczka, 1872: Pakistan

294. *Eremias guttulata* (Lichtenstein, 1823)
 Eremias guttulata watsonana (Stoliczka, 1872): India
295. *Eremias persica* Blanford, 1875: Pakistan
296. *Eremias velox* (Pallas, 1771): Pakistan
297. *Ophisops beddomei* (Jerdon, 1870): India
298. *Ophisops elegans* Ménétriés, 1832: Pakistan
299. *Ophisops jerdoni* Blyth, 1853: India, Pakistan
300. *Ophisops leschenaultii* (Milne-Edwards, 1829)
 Ophisops leschenaultii leschenaultii (Milne-Edwards, 1829): India
 Ophisops leschenaultii lankae (Deraniyagala, 1953): Sri Lanka
301. *Ophisops microlepis* Blanford, 1870: India
302. *Ophisops minor* (Deraniyagala, 1971)
 Ophisops minor minor (Deraniyagala, 1971): Sri Lanka
 Ophisops minor nictans Arnold, 1989: India
303. *Rhabderemias fasciata* (Blanford, 1874): Pakistan
304. *Rhabderemias scripta* (Strauch, 1867): Pakistan
305. *Scapteira acutirostris* Boulenger, 1887: Pakistan
306. *Scapteira aporosceles* (Alcock & Finn, 1896): Pakistan
307. *Takydromus haughtonianus* Jerdon, 1870: India
308. *Takydromus sexlineatus* Daudin, 1802
 Takydromus sexlineatus khasiensis (Boulenger, 1890): India

ANGUIDAE

309. *Ophisaurus gracilis* (Gray, 1845): India

VARANIDAE

310. *Varanus bengalensis* (Daudin, 1802): Bangladesh, Bhutan, India, Nepal, Pakistan, Sri Lanka
311. *Varanus flavescens* (Hardwicke & Gray, 1827): Bangladesh, India, Nepal, Pakistan
312. *Varanus griseus* (Daudin, 1803)
 Varanus griseus caspius (Eichwald, 1831): Pakistan
 Varanus griseus konicznyi Mertens, 1854: India, Pakistan
313. *Varanus salvator* (Laurenti, 1768)
 Varanus salvator salvator (Laurenti, 1768): Bangladesh, India
 Varanus salvator andamanensis Deraniyagala, 1944: India
 Varanus salvator karbaragoya Deraniyagala, 1947: Sri Lanka

SERPENTES

LEPTOTYPHLOPIDAE

314. *Leptotyphlops blanfordi* (Boulenger, 1890)
     Leptotyphlops blanfordi blanfordi (Boulenger, 1890): India, Pakistan
315. *Leptotyphlops macrorhynchus* (Jan, 1861): India, Pakistan

TYPHLOPIDAE

316. *Ramphotyphlops braminus* (Daudin, 1803): Bangladesh, Bhutan, India, Maldives, Nepal, Pakistan, Sri Lanka
317. *Typhlops acutus* (Duméril & Bibron, 1844): India
318. *Typhlops andamanensis* Stoliczka, 1871: India
319. *Typhlops beddomei* Boulenger, 1890: India
320. *Typhlops bothriorhynchus* Günther, 1864: India
321. *Typhlops ceylonicus* Smith, 1943: Sri Lanka
322. *Typhlops diardii* Schlegel, 1839
     Typhlops diardii diardii Schlegel, 1839: Bangladesh, India
323. *Typhlops jerdoni* Boulenger, 1890: India, Nepal
324. *Typhlops lankaensis* Taylor, 1947: Sri Lanka
325. *Typhlops leucomelas* Boulenger, 1890: Sri Lanka
326. *Typhlops loveridgei* Constable, 1949: India***
327. *Typhlops malcolmi* Taylor, 1947: Sri Lanka
328. *Typhlops mirus* Jan, 1860: Sri Lanka
329. *Typhlops oatesii* Boulenger, 1890: India
330. *Typhlops oligolepis* Wall, 1909: India
331. *Typhlops pammeces* Günther, 1864: India, Pakistan, Sri Lanka
332. *Typhlops porrectus* Stoliczka, 1871: Bangladesh, India, Pakistan, Sri Lanka
333. *Typhlops tenebrarum* Taylor, 1947: Sri Lanka
334. *Typhlops tenuicollis* (Peters, 1864): India
335. *Typhlops thurstoni* Boettger, 1890: India
336. *Typhlops tindalli* Smith, 1943: India
337. *Typhlops veddae* Taylor, 1947: Sri Lanka
338. *Typhlops violaceus* Taylor, 1947: Sri Lanka

XENOPELTIDAE

339. *Xenopeltis unicolor* Reinwardt in Boie, 1827: India

UROPELTIDAE

340. *Brachyophidium rhodogaster* Wall, 1921: India
341. *Cylindrophis maculata* (Linnaeus, 1754): Sri Lanka
342. *Melanophidium bilineatum* Beddome, 1870: India
343. *Melanophidium punctatum* Beddome, 1871: India
344. *Melanophidium wynaudense* (Beddome, 1863): India
345. *Platyplectrurus madurensis* Beddome, 1877
    Platyplectrurus madurensis madurensis Beddome, 1877: India
    Platyplectrurus madurensis ruhanae (Deraniyagala, 1954): Sri Lanka
346. *Platyplectrurus trilineatus* (Beddome, 1867): India
347. *Plectrurus aureus* Beddome, 1880: India
348. *Plectrurus canaricus* (Beddome, 1870): India
349. *Plectrurus guentheri* Beddome, 1863: India
350. *Plectrurus perroteti* Duméril & Bibron, 1854: India
351. *Pseudotyphlops philippinus* (Schlegel, 1839): Sri Lanka
352. *Rhinophis blythii* Kelaart, 1853: Sri Lanka
353. *Rhinophis dorsimaculatus* Deraniyagala, 1941: Sri Lanka
354. *Rhinophis drummondhayi* Wall, 1921: Sri Lanka
355. *Rhinophis fergusonianus* Boulenger, 1896: India
356. *Rhinophis oxyrhynchus* (Schneider, 1801): Sri Lanka
357. *Rhinophis philippinus* (Cuvier, 1829): Sri Lanka
358. *Rhinophis porrectus* Wall, 1921: Sri Lanka
359. *Rhinophis punctatus* Müller, 1832: Sri Lanka
360. *Rhinophis travancoricus* Boulenger, 1892: India
361. *Rhinophis trevelyana* (Kelaart, 1853): Sri Lanka
362. *Rhinophis tricolorata* Deraniyagala, 1975: Sri Lanka
363. *Teretrurus sanguineus* Beddome, 1867: India
364. *Uropeltis arcticeps* (Günther, 1875): India
365. *Uropeltis beddomii* (Günther, 1862): India
366. *Uropeltis broughami* (Beddome, 1878): India

367. *Uropeltis ceylanicus* Cuvier, 1829: India
368. *Uropeltis dindigalensis* (Beddome, 1877): India
369. *Uropeltis ellioti* (Gray, 1858): India
370. *Uropeltis liura* (Günther, 1875): India
371. *Uropeltis macrolepis* (Peters, 1861)
    Uropeltis macrolepis macrolepis (Peters, 1862): India
    Uropeltis macrolepis mahableshwarensis Chari, 1955: India
372. *Uropeltis macrorhyncha* (Beddome, 1877): India
373. *Uropeltis maculata* (Beddome, 1878): India
374. *Uropeltis melanogaster* (Gray, 1858): Sri Lanka
375. *Uropeltis myhendrae* Beddome, 1886: India
376. *Uropeltis nitida* (Beddome, 1878): India
377. *Uropeltis ocellata* (Beddome, 1863): India
378. *Uropeltis petersi* (Beddome, 1878): India
379. *Uropeltis phillipsi* (Nicholls, 1929): Sri Lanka
380. *Uropeltis phipsonii* (Mason, 1888): India
381. *Uropeltis pulneyensis* (Beddome, 1863): India
382. *Uropeltis rubrolineata* (Günther, 1875): India
383. *Uropeltis rubromaculatus* (Beddome, 1867): India
384. *Uropeltis ruhanae* Deraniyagala, 1954: Sri Lanka
385. *Uropeltis smithi* Gans, 1966: India
386. *Uropeltis woodmasoni* (Theobald, 1875): India

BOIDAE

387. *Eryx conica* (Schneider, 1801)
    Eryx conica conica (Schneider, 1801): Bangladesh, India, Pakistan
    Eryx conica brevis Deraniyagala, 1951: Sri Lanka
388. *Eryx johnii* (Russell, 1801)
    Eryx johnii johnii (Russell, 1801): India, Pakistan
    Eryx johnii persicus (Nikolsky, 1907): India, Pakistan
389. *Eryx tatarica* (Lichtenstein in Eversmann, 1823)
    Eryx tatarica vittatus Chernov, 1959: Pakistan
390. *Eryx whitakeri* Das, 1991: India

391. *Python molurus* (Linnaeus, 1758)
   Python molurus molurus (Linnaeus, 1758): Bhutan, India, Nepal, Pakistan, Sri Lanka
   Python molurus bivittatus Kuhl, 1820: Bangladesh, India
392. *Python reticulata* (Schneider, 1801): Bangladesh, India

ACROCHORDIDAE

393. *Acrochordus granulatus* (Schneider, 1799): Bangladesh, India, Pakistan, Sri Lanka

COLUBRIDAE

394. *Ahaetulla dispar* (Günther, 1864): India
395. *Ahaetulla fronticinctus* (Günther, 1858): India
396. *Ahaetulla nasutus* (Lacépède, 1789): Bangladesh, India, Nepal, Sri Lanka
397. *Ahaetulla perroteti* (Duméril & Bibron, 1854): India
398. *Ahaetulla prasina* (Reinwardt in Boie, 1827)
   Ahaetulla prasina prasina (Reinwardt in Boie, 1827): Bangladesh, Bhutan, India
399. *Ahaetulla pulverulentus* (Duméril & Bibron, 1854): India, Sri Lanka
400. *Amphiesma beddomei* (Günther, 1864): India
401. *Amphiesma khasiensis* (Boulenger, 1890): India
402. *Amphiesma modesta* (Günther, 1875): India
403. *Amphiesma monticola* (Jerdon, 1853): India
404. *Amphiesma nicobariensis* (Sclater, 1891): India
405. *Amphiesma parallela* (Boulenger, 1890): India, Nepal
406. *Amphiesma pealii* (Sclater, 1891): India
407. *Amphiesma platyceps* (Blyth, 1854): Bangladesh, Bhutan, India, Nepal, Pakistan
408. *Amphiesma sieboldii* (Günther, 1860): Bangladesh, India, Nepal, Pakistan
409. *Amphiesma stolata* (Linnaeus, 1758): Bangladesh, Bhutan, India, Nepal, Pakistan, Sri Lanka

410. *Amphiesma xenura* (Wall, 1907): India
411. *Argyrogena fasciolatus* (Shaw, 1802): Bangladesh, India, Nepal, Pakistan
412. *Aspidura brachyorrhos* (Boie, 1827): Sri Lanka
413. *Aspidura copei* Günther, 1864: Sri Lanka
414. *Aspidura deraniyagalae* Gans & Fetcho, 1982: Sri Lanka
415. *Aspidura drummondhayi* Boulenger, 1904: Sri Lanka
416. *Aspidura guentheri* Ferguson, 1876: Sri Lanka
417. *Aspidura trachyprocta* Cope, 1860: Sri Lanka
418. *Atretium schistosum* (Daudin, 1803): Bangladesh, India, Nepal, Sri Lanka
419. *Balanophis ceylonensis* (Günther, 1858): Sri Lanka
420. *Blythia reticulata* (Blyth, 1854): India
421. *Boiga andamanensis* (Wall, 1909): India
422. *Boiga barnesii* (Günther, 1869): Sri Lanka
423. *Boiga beddomei* (Wall, 1909): India, Sri Lanka
424. *Boiga ceylonensis* (Günther, 1858): India, Nepal, Sri Lanka
425. *Boiga cyanea* (Duméril, Bibron & Duméril, 1854): Bangladesh, India, Nepal
426. *Boiga cynodon* (Boie, 1827): Bangladesh, India
427. *Boiga dendrophila* (Boie, 1827)
   Boiga dendrophila subspecies (Boulenger, 1896): India
428. *Boiga dightoni* (Boulenger, 1894): India
429. *Boiga forsteni* (Duméril, Bibron & Duméril, 1854): India, Nepal, Sri Lanka
430. *Boiga gokool* (Gray, 1834): Bangladesh, Bhutan, India
431. *Boiga multifasciata* (Blyth, 1861): Bhutan, India, Nepal
432. *Boiga multomaculata* Reinwardt in Boie, 1827: Bangladesh
433. *Boiga nuchalis* (Günther, 1875): India, Nepal
434. *Boiga ochraceus* (Günther, 1868)
   Boiga ochraceus ochraceus (Günther, 1868): Bangladesh, Bhutan, India
   Boiga ochraceus stoliczkae (Wall, 1909): India, Nepal
   Boiga ochraceus walli Smith, 1943: India
435. *Boiga quincunciatus* (Wall, 1908): India

436. *Boiga trigonatus* (Schneider, 1802)
 Boiga trigonatus trigonatus (Schneider, 1802): Bangladesh, India, Nepal, Pakistan, Sri Lanka
 Boiga trigonatus melanocephalus (Annandale, 1904): Pakistan
437. *Calamaria pavimentata* Duméril, Bibron & Duméril, 1854: India
438. *Cantoria violacea* Girard, 1857: India
439. *Cerberus rhynchops* (Schneider, 1799)
 Cerberus rhynchops rhynchops (Schneider, 1799): Bangladesh, India, Pakistan, Sri Lanka
440. *Cercaspis carinata* (Kuhl, 1820): Sri Lanka
441. *Chrysopelea ornata* (Shaw, 1802)
 Chrysopelea ornata ornata (Shaw, 1802): Bangladesh, India
 Chrysopelea ornata sinhaleya Deraniyagala, 1945: Sri Lanka
442. *Chrysopelea paradisi* Boie, 1827: India
443. *Chrysopelea taprobanica* Smith, 1943: Sri Lanka
444. *Coluber bholanathi* Sharma, 1976: India
445. *Coluber gracilis* (Günther, 1862): India
446. *Coluber karelini* Brandt, 1838: Pakistan
447. *Coluber korros* Schlegel, 1837: India
448. *Coluber mucosus* (Linnaeus, 1758)
 Coluber mucosus mucosus (Linnaeus, 1758): Bangladesh, India, Nepal, Pakistan
 Coluber muscosus maximus (Deraniyagala, 1955): Sri Lanka
449. *Coluber nigromarginatus* (Blyth, 1854): Bangladesh, Bhutan, India, Nepal
450. *Coluber ravergieri* Ménétriés in De Filippi, 1832: Pakistan
451. *Coluber rhodorachis* (Jan, 1865): India, Pakistan
452. *Coluber ventromaculatus* Gray, 1834: India, Pakistan
453. *Coronella brachyurus* (Günther, 1866): India
454. *Dendrelaphis bifrenalis* (Boulenger, 1890): India, Sri Lanka
455. *Dendrelaphis caudolineolatus* (Günther, 1869): India, Sri Lanka
456. *Dendrelaphis cyanochloris* (Wall, 1921): Bangladesh, India
457. *Dendrelaphis gorei* (Wall, 1910): India
458. *Dendrelaphis grandoculis* (Boulenger, 1890): India
459. *Dendrelaphis humayuni* Tiwari & Biswas, 1973: India
460. *Dendrelaphis oliveri* (Taylor, 1950): Sri Lanka

461. *Dendrelaphis pictus* (Gmelin, 1789)
    Dendrelaphis pictus pictus (Gmelin, 1789): Bangladesh, India, Nepal
    Dendrelaphis pictus andamanensis (Smith, 1943): India
462. *Dendrelaphis tristis* (Daudin, 1803): Bangladesh, India, Nepal, Pakistan, Sri Lanka
463. *Dinodon gammiei* (Blanford, 1878): India
464. *Dinodon septentrionalis* (Günther, 1875)
    Dinodon septentrionalis septentrionalis (Günther, 1875): India
465. *Dryocalamus gracilis* (Günther, 1864): India, Sri Lanka
466. *Dryocalamus nympha* (Daudin, 1803): India, Sri Lanka
467. *Eirenis mcmahoni* (Wall, 1911): Pakistan
468. *Eirenis persica* (Anderson, 1872): Pakistan
469. *Elachistodon westermanni* Reinwardt, 1863: Bangladesh, India, Nepal
470. *Elaphe cantoris* (Boulenger, 1894): India, Nepal
471. *Elaphe flavolineata* (Schlegel, 1837): India
472. *Elaphe frenata* (Gray, 1853): India
473. *Elaphe helena* (Daudin, 1803)
    Elaphe helena helena (Daudin, 1803): Bangladesh, India, Nepal, Pakistan, Sri Lanka
    Elaphe helena monticollaris Schulz, 1992: India
474. *Elaphe hodgsonii* (Günther, 1860): India, Nepal
475. *Elaphe mandarina* (Cantor, 1842): India
476. *Elaphe porphyracea* (Cantor, 1839)
    Elaphe porphyracea porphyracea (Cantor, 1839): India
477. *Elaphe prasina* (Blyth, 1854): India
478. *Elaphe radiata* (Schlegel, 1837): Bangladesh, India, Nepal
479. *Elaphe taeniura* (Cope, 1861)
    Elaphe taeniura yunnanensis (Anderson, 1878): India
480. *Enhydris dussumieri* (Duméril & Bibron, 1854): India
481. *Enhydris enhydris* (Schneider, 1799): Bangladesh, India, Nepal
482. *Enhydris pakistanica* Mertens, 1959: Pakistan
483. *Enhydris sieboldii* Schlegel, 1837: Bangladesh, India, Nepal
484. *Fordonia leucobalia* (Schlegel, 1837): Bangladesh, India
485. *Gerardia prevostianus* (Eydoux & Gervais, 1837): Bangladesh, India, Sri Lanka

486. *Gonyosoma oxycephalus* (Boie, 1827): India
487. *Haplocercus ceylonensis* (Günther, 1858): Sri Lanka
488. *Homalopsis buccata* (Linnaeus, 1754): Bangladesh, India
489. *Liopeltis calamaria* (Günther, 1858): Bangladesh, India, Sri Lanka
490. *Liopeltis frenatus* (Günther, 1858): India
491. *Liopeltis nicobariensis* (Stoliczka, 1870): India
492. *Liopeltis rappi* (Günther, 1860): India, Nepal
493. *Liopeltis stoliczkae* (Sclater, 1891): India
494. *Lycodon aulicus* (Linnaeus, 1758): Bangladesh, India, Nepal, Pakistan, Sri Lanka
495. *Lycodon capucinus* (Boie, 1827): India, Maldives
496. *Lycodon fasciatus* Anderson, 1879: Bangladesh, India
497. *Lycodon flavomaculatus* (Wall, 1907): India
498. *Lycodon jara* (Shaw, 1802): Bangladesh, India, Nepal
499. *Lycodon laoensis* (Günther, 1864): India
500. *Lycodon mackinnoni* (Wall, 1906): India
501. *Lycodon osmanhilli* (Taylor, 1950): Sri Lanka
502. *Lycodon striatus* (Shaw, 1802)
    Lycodon striatus striatus (Shaw, 1802): India, Pakistan
    Lycodon striatus bicolor (Nikolsky, 1903): Pakistan
    Lycodon striatus sinhaleyus (Deraniyagala, 1955): Sri Lanka
503. *Lycodon tiwarii* Biswas & Sanyal, 1965: India
504. *Lycodon travancoricus* (Beddome, 1870): India
505. *Lytorhynchus maynardi* Alcock & Finn, 1896: Pakistan
506. *Lytorhynchus paradoxa* (Günther, 1875): Pakistan
507. *Lytorhynchus ridgewayi* Boulenger, 1887: Pakistan
508. *Macropisthodon plumbicolor* (Cantor, 1839)
    Macropisthodon plumbicolor plumbicolor (Cantor, 1839): Bangladesh, India, Pakistan
    Macropisthodon plumbicolor palabariya Deraniyagala, 1955: Sri Lanka
509. *Natrix tessellata* (Laurenti, 1768): Pakistan
510. *Oligodon affinis* Günther, 1862: India
511. *Oligodon albocincta* (Cantor, 1839): Bangladesh, India, Nepal
512. *Oligodon arnensis* (Shaw, 1802): Bangladesh, India, Nepal, Pakistan, Sri Lanka

513. *Oligodon brevicaudus* (Günther, 1862): India
514. *Oligodon calamarius* (Linnaeus, 1754): Sri Lanka
515. *Oligodon catenatus* (Blyth, 1854): India
516. *Oligodon cinereus* (Günther, 1864): Bangladesh, India
517. *Oligodon cyclurus* (Cantor, 1839)
   Oligodon cyclurus cyclurus (Cantor, 1839): Bangladesh, India
518. *Oligodon dorsalis* (Gray & Hardwicke, 1834): Bangladesh, India
519. *Oligodon dorsolateralis* (Wall, 1909): India
520. *Oligodon erythrogaster* Boulenger, 1907: India, Nepal
521. *Oligodon erythrorhachis* Wall, 1910: India
522. *Oligodon juglandifer* (Wall, 1909): India
523. *Oligodon kheriensis* Acharji & Ray, 1936: India
524. *Oligodon melaneus* Wall, 1909: India
525. *Oligodon melanozonatus* Wall, 1922: India
526. *Oligodon nikhili* Whitaker & Dattatri, 1982: India
527. *Oligodon sublineatus* Duméril, Bibron & Duméril, 1854: Sri Lanka
528. *Oligodon taeniolata* (Jerdon, 1853): Bangladesh, India, Pakistan, Sri Lanka
529. *Oligodon theobaldi* (Günther, 1868): India
530. *Oligodon travancoricum* Beddome, 1877: India
531. *Oligodon venustum* (Jerdon, 1853): India
532. *Oligidon woodmasoni* (Sclater, 1891): India
533. *Ophiodrys doriae* (Boulenger, 1888): India
534. *Pareas macularius* Theobald, 1868: Bangladesh, India
535. *Pareas monticola* (Cantor, 1839): Bangladesh, India
536. *Psammodynastes pulverulentus* (Boie, 1827): Bangladesh, India, Nepal
537. *Psammophis condanarus* (Merrem, 1820)
   Psammophis condanarus condanarus (Merrem, 1820): India, Nepal, Pakistan
538. *Psammophis leithii* Günther, 1869: India, Pakistan
539. *Psammophis lineolatus* (Brandt, 1838): Pakistan
540. *Psammophis longifrons* Boulenger, 1896: India
541. *Psammophis schokari* (Forsskål, 1775): India, Pakistan

542. *Pseudoxenodon macrops* (Blyth, 1854)
    Pseudoxenodon macrops macrops (Blyth, 1854): Bhutan, India, Nepal
543. *Rhabdophis himalayanus* (Günther, 1864): Bangladesh, Bhutan, India, Nepal
544. *Rhabdophis subminiatus* (Schlegel, 1837): Bangladesh, India, Nepal
545. *Rhabdops bicolor* (Blyth, 1854): India
546. *Rhabdops olivaceus* (Beddome, 1863): India
547. *Sibynophis bistrigatus* (Günther, 1868): India
548. *Sibynophis collaris* (Gray, 1853): India, Nepal
549. *Sibynophis sagittaria* (Cantor, 1839): Bangladesh, India, Nepal
550. *Sibynophis subpunctatus* (Duméril & Bibron, 1854): India, Sri Lanka
551. *Spalerosophis arenarius* (Boulenger, 1890): India, Pakistan
552. *Spalerosophis diadema* (Schlegel, 1837)
    Spalerosophis diadema diadema (Schlegel, 1837): India, Pakistan
    Spalerosophis diadema schiraziana (Jan, 1865): Pakistan
553. *Stoliczkaia khasiensis* Jerdon, 1870: India
554. *Telescopus rhinopoma* (Blanford, 1874): Pakistan
555. *Trachischium fusca* (Blyth, 1854): India, Nepal
556. *Trachischium guentheri* Boulenger, 1890: Bangladesh, Bhutan, India, Nepal
557. *Trachischium laeve* Peracca, 1904: India
558. *Trachischium monticola* (Cantor, 1839): Bangladesh, India
559. *Trachischium tenuiceps* (Blyth, 1854): Bangladesh, India, Nepal
560. *Xenochrophis asperrimus* (Boulenger, 1891): Sri Lanka
561. *Xenochrophis cerasogaster* (Cantor, 1839): Bangladesh, India, Nepal, Pakistan
562. *Xenochrophis flavipunctatum* (Hallowell, 1860)
    Xenochrophis flavipunctatum flavipunctatum (Hallowell, 1860): India
    Xenochrophis flavipunctatum schnurrenbergeri Kramer, 1977: Nepal
563. *Xenochrophis melanzostus* (Boie, 1826): India

564. *Xenochrophis piscator* (Schneider, 1799)
    Xenochrophis piscator piscator (Schneider, 1799): Bangladesh, Bhutan, India, Nepal, Pakistan, Sri Lanka
565. *Xenochrophis punctulatus* (Günther, 1858): India
566. *Xenochrophis sanctijohannis* (Boulenger, 1890): India, Pakistan
567. *Xenochropis trianguligerus* (Boie, 1827): India
568. *Xylophis perroteti* (Duméril & Bibron, 1854): India
569. *Xylophis stenorhynchus* (Günther, 1875): India

ELAPIDAE

570. *Bungarus andamanensis* Biswas & Sanyal, 1978: India
571. *Bungarus bungaroides* (Cantor, 1839): India
572. *Bungarus caeruleus* (Schneider, 1801): Bangladesh, India, Nepal, Pakistan, Sri Lanka
573. *Bungarus ceylonicus* Günther, 1864
    Bungarus ceylonicus ceylonicus Günther, 1864: Sri Lanka
    Bungarus ceylonicus karavala Deraniyagala, 1955: Sri Lanka
574. *Bungarus fasciatus* (Schneider, 1801): Bangladesh, India, Nepal
575. *Bungarus lividus* Cantor, 1839: Bangladesh, India
576. *Bungarus niger* Wall, 1908: Bangladesh, Bhutan, India
577. *Bungarus sindanus* Boulenger, 1897
    Bungarus sindanus sindanus Boulenger, 1897: India, Pakistan
    Bungarus sindanus razai Khan, 1985: Pakistan
    Bungarus sindanus walli Wall, 1907: Bangladesh, India, Nepali
578. *Calliophis beddomei* Smith, 1943: India
579. *Calliophis bibroni* (Jan, 1858): India
580. *Calliophis macclellandi* (Reinhardt, 1844)
    Calliophis macclellandi macclellandi (Reinhardt, 1944): India
    Calliophis macclellandi univirgatus (Günther, 1858): India, Nepal
581. *Calliophis melanurus* (Shaw, 1802)
    Calliophis melanurus melanurus (Shaw, 1802): Bangladesh, India
    Calliophis melanurus nigrescens Günther, 1862: India
    Calliophis melanurus sinhaleyus Deraniyagala, 1951: Sri Lanka
582. *Naja naja* (Linnaeus, 1758): Bangladesh, India, Nepal, Pakistan, Sri Lanka
583. *Naja kaouthia* Lesson, 1831: Bangladesh, India

584. *Naja oxiana* (Eichwald, 1831): India, Pakistan
585. *Ophiophagus hannah* (Cantor, 1836): Bangladesh, Bhutan, India, Nepal

HYDROPHIIDAE

586. *Astrotia stokesii* (Gray in Stokes, 1846): India, Pakistan, Sri Lanka
587. *Enhydrina schistosus* (Daudin, 1803): Bangladesh, India, Pakistan
588. *Hydrophis bituberculatus* Peters, "1872" 1873: Sri Lanka
589. *Hydrophis caerulescens* (Shaw, 1802): Bangladesh, India, Pakistan
590. *Hydrophis fasciatus* (Schneider, 1799)
   Hydrophis fasciatus fasciatus (Schneider, 1799): Bangladesh, India, Pakistan
591. *Hydrophis lapemoides* (Gray, 1849): India, Pakistan, Sri Lanka
592. *Hydrophis mamillaris* (Daudin, 1803): India, Pakistan, Sri Lanka
593. *Hydrophis nigrocinctus* Daudin, 1803: Bangladesh, India, Sri Lanka
594. *Hydrophis obscura* Daudin, 1803: Bangladesh, India, Sri Lanka
595. *Hydrophis ornatus* (Gray, 1842)
   Hydrophis ornatus ornatus (Gray, 1842): Bangladesh, India, Pakistan, Sri Lanka
596. *Hydrophis stricticollis* Günther, 1864: Bangladesh, India, Sri Lanka
597. *Kerilia jerdonii* Gray, 1849
   Kerilia jerdonii jerdonii Gray, 1849: India, Sri Lanka
598. *Lapemis curtus* Shaw, 1802: Bangladesh, India, Pakistan, Sri Lanka
599. *Laticauda colubrina* (Schneider, 1799): Bangladesh, India
600. *Laticauda laticaudata* (Linnaeus, 1758): Bangladesh, India
601. *Leioselasma cyanocinctus* (Daudin, 1803): Bangladesh, India, Pakistan, Sri Lanka
602. *Leiocephalus spiralis* (Shaw, 1802): India, Pakistan, Sri Lanka
603. *Microcephalophis cantoris* Günther, 1864: Bangladesh, India, Pakistan
604. *Microcephalophis gracilis* (Shaw, 1802): Bangladesh, India, Pakistan, Sri Lanka

605. *Pelamis platurus* (Linnaeus, 1766): India, Maldives, Pakistan, Sri Lanka
606. *Praescutata viperina* (Schmidt, 1852): India, Pakistan, Sri Lanka

VIPERIDAE

607. *Agkistrodon himalayanus* (Günther, 1864): India, Nepal, Pakistan
608. *Echis carinata* (Schneider, 1801)
    Echis carinata carinata (Schneider, 1801): India, Sri Lanka
    Echis carinata astolae Mertens, 1970: Pakistan
    Echis carinata multisquamatus Cherlin, 1981: Pakistan
    Echis carinata sochureki Stemmler, 1969: Bangladesh, India, Pakistan
609. *Eristicophis macmahoni* Alcock & Finn, 1896: India, Pakistan
610. *Hypnale hypnale* (Merrem, 1820): India, Sri Lanka
611. *Hypnale nepa* (Laurenti, 1768): Sri Lanka
612. *Hypnale walli* Gloyd, 1977: Sri Lanka
613. *Ovophis monticola* (Günther, 1864)
    Ovophis monticola monticola (Günther, 1864): Bangladesh, India, Nepal
614. *Protobothrops jerdonii* (Günther, 1875)
    Protobothrops jerdonii jerdonii (Günther, 1875): India
615. *Protobothrops mucrosquamatus* (Cantor, 1839): Bangladesh, India
616. *Trimeresurus albolabris* (Gray, 1842)
    Trimeresurus albolabris septentrionalis Kramer, 1977: Bangladesh, India, Nepal
617. *Trimeresurus cantori* (Blyth, 1846): India
618. *Trimeresurus erythrurus* (Cantor, 1839): Bangladesh, India, Nepal
619. *Trimeresurus gramineus* (Shaw, 1802): Bangladesh, India, Nepal
620. *Trimeresurus huttoni* Smith, 1949: India
621. *Trimeresurus labialis* Fitzinger, 1861: India
622. *Trimeresurus macrolepis* Beddome, 1862: India
623. *Trimeresurus malabaricus* (Jerdon, 1854): India
624. *Trimeresurus popeiorum* Smith, 1937: Bangladesh, India
625. *Trimeresurus purpureomaculatus* (Gray & Hardwicke, 1830)
    Trimeresurus purpureomaculatus andersoni Theobald, 1868: India

626. *Trimeresurus stejnegeri* Schmidt, 1925
    Trimeresurus stejnegeri yunnanensis Schmidt, 1925: India, Nepal
627. *Trimeresurus strigatus* Gray, 1842: India
628. *Trimeresurus trigonocephala* (Sonnini & Latreille, 1801): Sri Lanka
629. *Vipera lebetina* (Linnaeus, 1758)
    Vipera lebetina obtusa Dvigubsky, 1832: Pakistan
630. *Vipera persicus* (Duméril & Bibron, 1854)
    Vipera persicus persicus (Duméril & Bibron, 1854): Pakistan
631. *Vipera russelii* (Shaw & Nodden, 1797)
    Vipera russelii russelii (Shaw & Nodden, 1797): Bangladesh, India, Pakistan, Sri Lanka

TABLE 2

TAXONOMIC COMPOSITION AND ENDEMICITY OF THE REPTILES OF SOUTH ASIA

Families	No. of genera	No. of species	No. of endemics	% endemicity
CROCODILIA				
Crocodylidae	1	2	0	0.0
Gavialiidae	1	1	0	0.0
TESTUDINES				
Dermochelyidae	1	1	0	0.0
Cheloniidae	4	4	0	0.0
Bataguridae	10	16	11	68.8
Testudinidae	4	5	2	40.0
Trionychidae	4	7	5	71.4
SAURIA				
Gekkonidae	26	97	76	78.4
Agamidae	21	68	48	70.6
Chamaeleonidae	1	1	1	100.0
Dibamidae	1	1	0	0.0
Scincidae	19	86	70	81.4
Lacertidae	6	19	8	42.1
Anguidae	1	1	1	100.0
Varanidae	1	4	1	25.0
SERPENTES				
Leptotyphlopidae	1	2	0	0.0
Typhlopidae	2	23	19	82.6
Xenopeltidae	1	1	0	0.0
Uropeltidae	9	47	47	100.0
Boidae	2	6	2	33.0
Acrochordidae	1	1	0	0.0
Colubridae	45	176	95	54.0
Elapidae	4	16	10	62.5
Hydrophiidae	11	21	0	0.0
Viperidae	8	25	13	52.0
TOTAL	185	632	411	63.7

TABLE 3

SPECIES RICHNESS OF REPTILES OF SOUTH ASIA AND THEIR FOCUS

Numbers in parentheses are endemic species. Marine and estuerine species excluded. Introduced species (*Lissemys punctata* in the Andamans) not included.

Zone	crocodiles	turtles	lizards	snakes	total
AN	1	0	22	25	48(10)
DC	1	7	29	40	77(5)
EG	3	8	32	41	84(12)
HM	2	15	33	96	146(22)
NE	2	19	32	95	148(35)
NI	1	1	22	22	46(7)
NW	2	8	71	36	117(36)
SL	2	3	67	78	148(80)
TH	0	1	47	41	89(19)
WG	1	5	65	94	165(88)

TABLE 4

ENDEMIC GENERA AND NUMBER OF ENDEMIC REPTILE SPECIES IN SOUTH ASIA

Endemic genera	No. of species	AN	DC	EG	HM	NE	NI	NW	SL	TH	WG
TESTUDINES											
Geoclemys	(1)	-	-	-	+	+	-	+	-	-	-
Hardella	(1)	-	-	-	+	+	-	+	-	-	-
Aspideretes	(4)	-	+	+	+	+	-	+	-	+	+
LACERTILIA											
Bufoniceps	(1)	-	-	-	-	-	-	+	-	-	-
Calodactylodes	(2)	-	-	+	-	-	-	-	+	-	-
Geckoella	(6)	-	-	+	-	-	-	-	+	-	+
Teratolepis	(2)	-	+	-	-	-	-	+	-	-	-
Ceratophora	(3)	-	-	-	-	-	-	-	+	-	-
Coryphophylax	(1)	+	-	-	-	-	+	-	-	-	-
Lyriocephalus	(1)	-	-	-	-	-	-	-	+	-	-
Mictopholis	(1)	-	-	-	-	+	-	-	-	-	-
Otocryptis	(2)	-	-	-	-	-	-	-	+	-	+
Psammophilus	(2)	-	+	+	-	-	-	-	-	-	+
Sitana	(1)	-	+	+	-	-	-	+	+	-	-
Barkudia	(1)	-	-	+	-	-	-	-	-	-	-
Chalcidoseps	(1)	-	-	-	-	-	-	-	+	-	-
Lankascincus	(6)	-	-	-	-	-	-	-	+	-	-
Nessia	(8)	-	-	-	-	-	-	-	+	-	-
Ristella	(4)	-	-	-	-	-	-	-	-	-	+
Sepsophis	(1)	-	-	+	-	-	-	-	-	-	-
SERPENTES											
Brachyophidium	(1)	-	- -	-	-	-	-	-	-	-	+
Melanophidium	(3)	-	-	-	-	-	-	-	-	-	+
Platyplectrurus	(2)	-	-	-	-	-	-	-	+	-	+
Plectrurus	(4)	-	-	-	-	-	-	-	-	-	+
Pseudotyphlops	(1)	-	-	-	-	-	-	-	+	-	-
Rhinophis	(11)	-	-	-	-	-	-	-	+	-	+
Teretrurus	(1)	-	-	-	-	-	-	-	-	-	+

TABLE 4, CONTINUED

Endemic genera	No. of species	AN	DC	EG	HM	NE	NI	NW	SL	TH	WG
Uropeltis	(23)	-	-	+	-	-	-	-	+	-	+
Argyrogena	(1)	-	+	-	+	-	-	+	-	+	-
Aspidura	(6)	-	-	-	-	-	-	-	+	-	-
Balanophis	(1)	-	-	-	-	-	-	-	+	-	-
Cercaspis	(1)	-	-	-	-	-	-	-	+	-	-
Elachistodon	(1)	-	-	-	+	-	-	-	-	-	-
Haplocercus	(1)	-	-	-	-	-	-	-	+	-	-
Trachischium	(5)	-	-	-	+	+	-	-	-	+	-
Xylophis	(2)	-	-	-	-	-	-	-	-	-	+
Hypnale	(3)	-	-	-	-	-	-	-	+	-	+

TABLE 5

AFFINITIES OF THE NON-ENDEMIC REPTILE GENERA IN SOUTH ASIA

Distribution / estuarine species excluded.
*   =   excluding *Cnemaspis boiei*, whose distribution is unknown
**   =   estuarine species

Genera	No. of species	AN	DC	EG	HM	NE	NI	NW	SL	TH	WG
TURKOMANIAN-CENTRAL ASIAN											
Ablepharus	(2)	-	-	-	-	-	-	+	-	-	-
Alsophylax	(1)	-	-	-	-	-	-	-	-	+	-
Crossobamon	(2)	-	-	-	-	-	-	+	-	-	-
Eremias	(4)	-	-	-	-	-	-	+	-	+	-
Laudakia	(8)	-	+	-	-	-	-	+	-	+	-
Lytorhynchus	(3)	-	-	-	-	-	-	+	-	-	-
Phrynocephalus	(8)	-	-	-	-	-	-	+	-	+	-
Rhabderemias	(2)	-	-	-	-	-	-	-	-	+	-
Scapteira	(2)	-	-	-	-	-	-	+	-	-	-
Teratoscincus	(2)	-	-	-	-	-	-	+	-	-	-
AFRO-MEDITERRANEAN											
Acanthodactylus	(3)	-	-	-	-	-	-	+	-	+	-
Agamura	(3)	-	-	-	-	-	-	+	-	-	-
Bunopus	(1)	-	-	-	-	-	-	+	-	-	-
Chalcides	(2)	-	-	-	-	-	-	+	-	-	+
Chamaeleo	(1)	-	+	+	-	-	-	+	+	-	-
Coronella	(1)	-	+	-	-	-	-	-	-	-	-
Echis	(1)	-	+	+	-	-	-	+	+	-	-
Eryx	(3)	-	+	+	-	-	-	+	+	-	+
Eublepharis	(2)	-	+	+	-	-	-	+	-	-	-
Geochelone	(1)	-	+	+	-	-	-	+	+	-	+
Leptotyphlops	(2)	-	-	-	-	-	-	+	-	+	-
Microgecko	(1)	-	-	-	-	-	-	+	-	-	-
Natrix	(1)	-	-	-	-	-	-	+	-	-	-
Ophisops	(6)	-	+	+	-	-	-	+	+	-	+
Pristurus	(1)	-	-	-	-	-	-	+	-	-	-
Ptyodactylus	(1)	-	-	-	-	-	-	+	-	-	-
Scincus	(1)	-	-	-	-	-	-	+	-	-	-
Telescopus	(1)	-	-	-	-	-	-	+	-	-	-

TABLE 5, CONTINUED

Genera	No. of species	AN	DC	EG	HM	NE	NI	NW	SL	TH	WG
Testudo	(1)	-	-	-	-	-	-	-	-	+	-
Trapelus	(4)	-	-	-	-	-	-	+	-	-	-
Tropiocolotes	(1)	-	-	-	-	-	-	+	-	-	-
Uromastyx	(2)	-	-	-	-	-	-	+	-	-	-
Vipera	(3)	-	+	+	-	-	-	+	+	-	+

TIBETO-YUNNANESE

Agkistrodon	(1)	-	-	-	-	-	-	+	-	+	-
Cuora	(1)	-	-	-	-	+	+	-	-	-	-
Cyrtopodion	(4)	-	-	-	-	-	-	+	-	+	-
Dinodon	(2)	-	-	-	+	+	-	-	-	-	-
Eumeces	(4)	-	+	-	-	-	-	+	-	+	-
Gekko	(3)	+	-	+	+	+	+	+	-	-	-
Japalura	(6)	-	-	-	+	+	-	-	-	+	-
Protobothrops	(2)	-	-	-	-	+	-	-	-	-	-
Pseudoxenodon	(1)	-	-	-	+	+	-	-	-	-	-
Takydromus	(2)	-	-	-	-	+	-	-	-	-	-

INDO-MALAYAN

*Acrochordus***	(1)	-	-	-	-	-	-	-	-	-	-
Amphiesma	(11)	-	+	+	+	+	+	+	+	+	+
*Batagur***	(1)	-	-	-	-	-	-	-	-	-	-
Bronchocela	(3)	-	-	-	-	-	+	-	-	-	-
Calamaria	(1)	-	-	-	-	+	-	-	-	-	-
*Cantoria***	(1)	+	-	-	-	-	-	-	-	-	-
*Cerberus***	(1)	-	-	-	-	-	-	-	-	-	-
Chrysopelea	(3)	+	-	+	-	+	-	-	+	-	+
Cnemaspis	(14)*	-	-	-	-	-	-	-	+	-	+
Cophotis	(1)	-	-	-	-	-	-	-	+	-	-
Cosymbotus	(1)	-	-	-	+	+	+	-	+	+	-
Crocodylus	(2)	+	+	+	+	+	+	+	+	-	+
Cyclemys	(1)	-	-	-	+	+	-	-	-	-	-
Cylindrophis	(1)	-	-	-	-	-	-	-	+	-	-
Dasamia	(1)	-	-	-	-	-	+	-	-	-	-
Dasia	(4)	+	-	-	-	-	+	-	+	-	+
Dibamus	(1)	-	-	-	-	-	+	-	-	-	-
Draco	(2)	-	-	-	-	-	-	-	-	-	+
Dryocalamus	(2)	-	-	+	-	-	-	-	+	-	+
Enhydris	(4)	-	+	+	+	+	-	+	+	+	+
Gehyra	(1)	+	-	+	-	-	-	-	+	-	+

TABLE 5, CONTINUED

Genera	No. of species	AN	DC	EG	HM	NE	NI	NW	SL	TH	WG
Gonydactylus	(15)	+	-	-	+	+	-	+	+	+	-
Gonyosoma	(1)	+	-	-	-	-	+	-	-	-	-
Hemiphyllo-dactylus	(1)	-	-	-	-	-	+	-	+	-	-
Lipinia	(2)	+	-	-	-	-	+	-	-	-	-
Lygosoma	(10)	-	+	+	+	+	-	+	+	+	+
Macropisthodon	(1)	-	-	-	+	+	-	+	+	+	+
Manouria	(1)	-	-	-	-	+	-	-	-	-	-
Naja	(3)	+	+	+	+	+	+	+	+	+	+
Ophiophagus	(1)	+	-	+	+	+	+	-	-	-	+
Ophisaurus	(1)	-	-	-	+	+	-	-	-	-	-
Psammodynastes	(1)	-	-	+	+	+	-	-	-	-	-
Pseudocalotes	(1)	-	-	-	-	+	-	-	-	-	-
Ptychozoon	(1)	+	-	-	-	-	+	-	-	-	-
Python	(2)	-	+	+	+	+	+	+	+	+	+
Ramphotyphlops	(1)	+	+	+	+	+	+	+	+	+	+
Rhabdophis	(2)	-	-	-	+	+	-	-	-	-	-
Sphenomorphus	(9)	+	-	-	+	+	-	+	-	-	+
Tropidophorus	(1)	-	-	-	-	+	-	-	-	-	-
Varanus	(4)	+	+	+	+	+	+	+	+	+	+
Xenochrophis	(7)	+	+	+	+	+	+	+	+	+	+
Xenopeltis	(1)	+	-	-	-	-	+	-	-	-	-

INDIAN RADIATION

Ahaetulla	(6)	-	+	+	+	+	-	-	+	-	+
Bungarus	(9)	+	+	+	+	+	+	+	+	+	+
Calotes	(16)	+	+	+	+	+	+	+	+	+	+
Gavialis	(1)	-	-	+	+	+	-	+	-	-	-
Hemidactylus	(21)	+	+	+	+	+	+	+	+	+	+
Kachuga	(6)	-	+	+	+	+	-	+	-	+	-
Lissemys	(1)	-	+	+	+	+	-	+	+	+	+
Melanochelys	(2)	-	+	-	+	+	-	-	+	-	-
Rhabdops	(2)	-	-	-	-	+	-	-	-	-	+
Salea	(3)	-	-	-	-	+	-	-	-	-	+
Spalerosophis	(2)	-	+	-	-	-	-	+	-	-	-
Teratolepis	(2)	-	+	-	-	-	-	+	-	-	-

OTHER FOREIGN ELEMENTS (OCEANIC/PHILIPPINES)

Lepidodactylus	(1)	+	-	-	-	-	+	-	+	-	-
Phelsuma	(1)	+	-	-	-	-	-	-	-	-	-

TABLE 5, CONTINUED

Genera	No. of species	AN	DC	EG	HM	NE	NI	NW	SL	TH	WG
TRANSITIONAL											
Asiocolotes	(1)	-	-	-	-	-	-	+	-	-	-
Atretium	(1)	-	+	+	-	-	-	-	+	-	+
Blythia	(1)	-	-	-	-	+	-	-	-	-	-
Boiga	(16)	+	+	+	+	+	+	+	+	+	+
Calliophis	(4)	-	+	-	+	+	-	-	+	-	+
Chitra	(1)	-	+	+	+	+	-	+	-	-	-
Dendrelaphis	(9)	+	+	+	+	+	+	+	+	+	+
Eirenis	(2)	-	-	-	-	-	-	+	-	-	-
Eristicophis	(1)	-	-	-	-	-	-	+	-	-	-
Indotestudo	(2)	-	-	+	+	+	-	-	-	-	+
Liopeltis	(5)	-	-	-	+	+	+	-	+	-	-
Lycodon	(11)	+	+	+	+	+	+	+	+	+	+
Morenia	(1)	-	-	-	+	+	-	-	-	-	-
Oligodon	(22)	+	+	+	+	+	+	+	+	+	+
Ophiomorus	(3)	-	-	-	-	-	-	+	-	-	-
Oriocalotes	(1)	-	-	-	-	+	-	-	-	-	-
Pareas	(2)	-	-	-	+	+	-	-	-	-	-
Pyxidea	(1)	-	-	-	-	+	-	-	-	-	-
Scincella	(6)	-	-	-	+	+	+	-	-	+	+
Sibynophis	(4)	-	+	-	+	+	+	-	+	-	+
Stoliczkaia	(1)	-	-	-	-	+	-	-	-	-	-
Tenuidactylus	(6)	-	-	-	-	-	-	+	-	-	-
Trimeresurus	(14)	+	-	-	+	+	+	-	+	-	+
Typhlops	(22)	+	+	+	+	+	-	+	+	+	+
UNKNOWN											
Coluber	(9)	-	+	+	+	+	-	+	+	+	+
Elaphe	(10)	+	+	+	+	+	+	+	+	+	+
*Fordonia***	(1)	-	-	-	-	-	-	-	-	-	-
Geoemyda	(1)	-	-	-	-	-	-	-	-	-	+
*Gerardia***	(1)	-	-	-	-	-	-	-	-	-	-
Homalopsis	(1)	-	-	-	-	+	-	-	-	-	-
Mabuya	(20)	+	+	+	+	+	+	+	+	+	+
Ophiodrys	(1)	-	-	-	-	+	-	-	-	-	-
*Pelochelys***	(1)	-	-	-	-	-	-	-	-	-	-
Psammophis	(5)	-	+	+	-	-	-	-	-	-	+

TABLE 6

REPRESENTATION OF EXTRALIMITAL REPTILE GENERA IN THE FOUR NORTHERN ZONES OF SOUTH ASIA

Extralimital faunal links	NW	TH	HM	NE
PALAEARCTIC	28	4	0	0
Turkomanian-Central Asian	9	3	0	0
Afro-Mediterranean	19	1	0	0
ORIENTAL	19	16	22	34
Tibeto-Yunnanese	4	4	4	7
Indo-Malayan	8	8	11	18
Indian	7	4	7	8
TRANSITIONAL	11	6	12	14

TABLE 7

SPECIES PAIRS OF REPTILES (BASED ON ECOLOGICAL SIMILARITY) FROM SOUTH ASIA AND ADJACENT REGIONS, SHOWING SISTER SPECIES BOUNDARIES AND PRESUMED MODE OF SPECIATION

Species-pair	Boundary	Speciation mode*
1. *Morenia petersi - M. occelata*	Naga-Arakan	Disp
2. *Geochelone elegans - G. platynota*	Naga-Arakan	Disp
3. *Indotestudo elongata - I. forstenii*	Deccan	Vic
4. *Lissemys punctata - L. scutata*	Naga-Arakan	Disp
5. *Aspideretes leithii - A. hurum*	Plains north of Godavari	Disp
6. *Callodactylodes aureus - C. illingworthi*	Palk Northern Sri Lanka	Vic
7. *Crossobamon eversmanni - C. orientalis*	Kirthar	Disp
8. *Eublepharis hardwickii - E. macularius*	Ganga	Disp
9. *Gekko smithii - G. verreauxi*	10° Channel + Preparis	Disp
10. *Draco blanfordi - D. dussumieri*	Deccan	Vic
11. *Otocryptis beddomeii - O. wiegmanni*	Palk Northern Sri Lanka	Vic
12. *Salea anamallayana - S. kakhiensis*	Deccan	Vic
13. *Salea horsfieldii - S. kakhiensis*	Deccan	Vic
14. *Uromastyx asmussi - U. hardwickii*	Kirthar	Disp
15. *Ophiomorus blanfordi - O. raithmai*	Kirthar	Disp
16. *Ptyctolaemus gularis - P. phuwuanensis*	Naga-Arakan	Disp
17. *Cylindrophis maculatus - C. ruffus*	Deccan + Palk + Northern Sri Lanka	Vic
18. *Eryx conica - E. whitakeri*	Western Ghats	Ref
19. *Atretium schistosum - A. yunnanensis*	Naga-Mishmi	Disp
20. *Chrysopelea ornatus - C. paradisi*	Naga-Arakan	Disp
21. *Dinodon gammiei - D. septentrionale*	Brahmaputra	Disp
22. *Gonyosoma oxycephalus - G. enganensis*	Great Channel	Disp
23. *Stoliczkaia khasiensis - S. borneensis*	Naga-Arakan	Vic
24. *Rhabdops bicolor - R. olivaceus*	Deccan	Vic
25. *Naja naja - N. kaouthia*	Plains of north-peninsular India	Ref
26. *Naja naja - N. oxiana*	Northwestern Highlands	Vic

* Disp = Dispersal; Ref = Refugial; Vic = Vicariance

Chapter 6

SUMMARY

1. The reptile fauna of south Asia is rich at both the generic and specific levels, with a total of 631 species of crocodiles, turtles, lizards, and snakes in 185 genera. Of this fauna, 39 genera (21%) and 402 species (63.7%) are endemic to the region.

2. Distinctive Indian radiation is displayed by several genera of non-squamate and squamate reptiles. With the exception of one widespread genus, these are confined to the mesic forests of the Western Ghats and/or Sri Lanka. Few taxa of Indian origin are found extralimitally, and it is hypothesized that the autochthonous fauna of the Indian region is largely of the non-emigrant type, the allochthonous elements from Indo-Malaya within the region, however, emigrants, utilizing habitats and filling niches not used by the local reptile fauna.

3. Ten well-demarcated physiogeographic zones are identifiable within the south Asian region, and species diversity is highest in zones supporting tropical moist forests, including Sri Lanka, Western Ghats, Northeast, and Himalayas. The snake faunas of these forested zones are much more speciose than the saurofaunas. The pattern is reversed in the more xeric regions of the Northwest and the Trans-Himalayas, where certain highly specialized lizards appear to have replaced some groups of snakes.

4. The Western Ghats and Sri Lanka are sister areas, sharing many genera. The two rainforest reptile faunas of the two regions are separated by a shallow saltwater stretch and a fairly extensive dry savannah-type vegetation.

5. The Northeast and the Himalayas are sister areas, showing higher generic overlap than with the Trans-Himalayas. The first two regions are separated by a river (Brahmaputra) and its associated valleys.

6. The Eastern Ghats is a sister area of the Deccan in faunal similarity. At least part of the reason may be linked to human activities, some of the species common to these zones being human-commensals that characterize heavily distributed areas.

7. Zones abutting continental areas show high extralimital or allochthonous elements. The fauna of the Northwest shows this pattern best, its affinities closer to the Afro-Mediterranean fauna than to the Oriental one. The Trans-Himalayas show Turkomanian and Central-Asian links. The Northeast and Himalayas display Indo-Malayan elements, as do the Bay Islands.

8. The dispersal speciation mode accounted for 53.9% of the 26 cases of sister species' evolution examined, and was correlated to hill ranges, plains, rivers, and deep saltwater breaks; the vicariance mode accounted for 38.5%, and was associated with topographic/climatic and shallow saltwater breaks; and rarest of the speciation modes, the refugial mode, accounted for 7.7% of the cases, and was linked to hill ranges and sharp xeric-mesic gradients.

9. Marked discontinuous ranges are evidenced by several species of reptiles, although the allopatric populations in many cases are morphologically distinct. Future systematic, ecological and biogeographic work is likely to result in some of these populations being elevated to subspecies, and in some cases, even to the rank of species, thereby increasing the known number of reptile species recorded from south Asia.

REFERENCES

Acharji, M. N., & M. B. Kripalani. 1951. On a collection of Reptilia and Batrachia from the Kangra and Kulu Valleys, western Himalayas. *Rec. Indian Mus.* 44:175–184.

Agrawal, H. P. 1979. A check-list of reptiles of Himachal Pradesh, India. *Indian J. Zootomy* 20:115–124.

Annandale, N. 1904. Contributions to Oriental herpetology I- The lizards of the Andamans, with the description of a new gecko and a note on the reproduced tail in *Ptychozoon homalocephalum*. *J. Asiatic Soc. Bengal* 63:12–22.

Annandale, N. 1905. Additions to the collection of Oriental snakes in the Indian Museum. -Part 2. - Specimens from the Andamans and Nicobars. *J. Asiatic Soc. Bengal* 64:173–176.

Arnold, E. N. 1992. The Rajasthan toad-headed lizard, *Phrynosoma laungwalaensis* (Reptilia: Agamidae), represents a new genus. *J. Herpetol.* 26:467–472.

Arnold, E, N., & A. E. Leviton. 1977. A revision of the lizard genus *Scincus* (Reptilia: Scincidae). *Bull. Brit. Mus. (nat. Hist.) Zool.* 31(5):189–248.

Ashton, P. S., & C. V. S. Gunatilleke. 1987. New light on the plant geography of Ceylon. I. Historical plant geography. *J. Biogeog.* 14:249–285.

Auffenberg, W., & H. Rehman. 1991. Studies on Pakistan reptiles. Pt. 1. The genus *Echis* (Viperidae). *Bull. Florida Mus. nat. Hist. Biol. Sci.* 35:263–314.

Auffenberg, W., & H. Rehman. 1993. Studies on Pakistan reptiles. Pt. 3. *Calotes versicolor. Asiatic Herpetol. Res.* 5:14–30.

Auffenberg, W., & H. Rehman. 1995 *Calotes versicolor nigrigularis* Auffenberg and Rehman a junior primary homonym. *Asiatic Herpetol. Res.* 6:27.

Bartlett, A. S., & E. S. Barghoorn. 1973. Phytogeographic history of the isthmus of Panama during the past 12,000 years (a history of vegetation, climate and sea-level change). *In:* Vegetation and vegetational history of northern Latin America. A. Graham (ed). Elsevier, Amsterdam.

Bauer, A. M., & R. Günther. 1992. A preliminary report on the reptile fauna of the Kingdom of Bhutan with the description of a new species of scincid lizard (Reptilia: Scincidae). *Asiatic Herpteol. Res.* 4:23–36.

Biswas, S., & D. P. Sanyal. 1977a. Notes on the Reptilia collection from the Great Nicobar Island during the Great Nicobar Expedition, 1966. *Rec. Zool. Surv. India* 72:107–124.

Biswas, S., & D. P. Sanyal. 1977b. Fauna of Rajasthan, India, Part: Reptilia. *Rec. Zool. Surv. India* 73:247–269.

Biswas, S., & D. P. Sanyal. 1980. A report on the Reptilia fauna of Andaman and Nicobar Islands in the collection of the Zoological Survey of India. *Rec. Zool. Surv. India* 77:255–292.

Bloom, A. L. 1983. Sea level and coastal morphology of the United States through the Late Wisconsin Glacial maximum. *In:* Late-Quaternary Environments of the United States. Vol. I. The Late Pleistocene. S. C. Porter (ed). University of Minnesota Press, Minneapolis.

Burger, W. L. 1971. Genera of pitvipers (Serpentes: Crotalidae). Ph.D. Dissertation, University of Kansas.

Cadle, J. E., H. C. Dessauer, C. Gans, & D. F. Gartside. 1990. Phylogenetic relationships and molecular evolution in uropeltid snakes (Serpentes: Uropeltidae): allozyme and albumin immunology. *Biol. J. Linn. Soc.* 40:293–320.

Carlquist, S. 1965. Island life. Natural History Press, New York.

Champion, H. G., & S. K. Seth. 1968. A revised survey of the forest types of India. Government of India Printing, Delhi.

Cheetham, A. H., & J. E. Hazel. 1969. Binary (presence-absence) similarity coefficients. *J. Paleont.* 43:1130–1136.

Choudhury, A. 1993. Potential biosphere reserves in Assam (India). *Tigerpaper* 20:2–8.

Colbert, E. H. 1933. The presence of Tubulidentates in the Middle Siwalik beds of northern India. *Amer. Mus. Nov.* (604):1–10.

Collins, N. M., J. A. Sayer, & T. C. Whitmore. (eds) 1991. The conservation atlas of tropical forests: Asia and the Pacific. Macmillan Press Ltd., London and Basingstroke.

Cooray, P. G. 1967. An introduction to the geology of Ceylon. *Spolia Zeylanica* 31:1–324.

Crowell, K. L. 1986. A comparison of relict versus equilibrium models for insular mammals of the Gulf of Maine. *Biol. J. Linn. Soc.* 28:37–64.

Daniels, R. J. R., & N. M. Ishwar. 1993. Herpetofauna of the wetlands of the Eastern Ghats — A status survey. Report to the Asian Wetland Bureau, Malaysia. Mimeo. 26 pg.

Darlington, P. J. 1959. Area, climate, and evolution. *Evol.* 13:488–510.

Das, I. 1988. On a collection of some Amphibia and Chelonia from Meghalaya. *Hamadryad* 13:17–19.

Das, I. 1991. Colour guide to the turtles and tortoises of the Indian Subcontinent. R & A Publishing, Portishead.

Das, I., & P. C. H. Pritchard. 1990. Intergradation between *Melanochelys trijuga trijuga* and *M. trijuga coronata* (Testudines: Emydidae: Batagurinae). *Asiatic Herpetol. Res.* 3:52–53.

Das, I., & R. Whitaker. 1990. Herpetological investigations in the Western Ghats, south India. Part I. The Vanjikadavu and Nadukani forests, Kerala. *Hamadryad* 15:6–9.

Deraniyagala, P. E. P. 1953. A colored atlas of some vertebrates from Ceylon. Vol. 2. Tetrapod reptiles. The Ceylon Government Press, Colombo.

de Silva, A. 1990. Colour guide to the snakes of Sri Lanka. R & A Publishing Limited, Portishead.

de Silva, P. H. D. H. 1980. Snake fauna of Sri Lanka with special reference to skull, dentition and venom in snakes. National Museum of Sri Lanka, Colombo.

Dilger, W. C. 1952. The Brij Hypothesis as an explanation for the tropical faunal similarities between the Western Ghats and the eastern Himalayas, Assam, Burma, and Malaya. *Evolution* 67:125–127.

Djao, E.-M., & Y.-M. Jiang. 1977. A survey of reptiles in Xizang Autonomous Region, with faunal analysis and descriptions of new forms. *Acta Zoologica Sinica* 23(1):64–71, 2 plates. [In Chinese with English abstract.]

Duda, P. L., & D. N. Sahi. 1977. An uptodate checklist of herpetiles of Jammu and Kashmir. *Univ. Rev.* 6:1–7.
Duellman, W. E. 1978. The biology of an equatorial herpetofauna in Amazonian Ecuador. *Misc. Publ. Mus. nat. Hist. Univ. Kansas* 65:1–352.
Durand, H. M. 1836. Specimens of the *Hippopotamus* and other fossil genera of the Sub-Himalayas in the Dadupur collection. *Asiat. Res.* 19:54–59.
Endler, J. A. 1982. Problems in distinguishing historical from ecological factors in biogeography. *Amer. Zool.* 22:441–452.
Erdelen, W. 1989. Aspects of the biogeography of Sri Lanka. *In*: Forschungen auf Ceylon. III. U. Schweinfurth (ed). pp: 73–100. Franz Steiner Verlag, Stuttgart.
Erdelen, W. 1993. Human impact on tropical rain forest in Sri Lanka. Paper presented at the International Conference on Tropical Rainforest Research: Current Issues. 9–17 April, 1993. Bandar Seri Begawan.
Erdelen, W., & C. Preu, 1990. Quaternary coastal and vegetation dynamics in the Palk Strait region, South Asia — The evidence and hypotheses. *In*: Vegetation and erosion. pp: 491–504. J. B. Thornes (ed). John Wiley and Sons Ltd., London and New York.
Fernando, S. N. U. 1968. The natural vegetation of Ceylon. Swabasha Printers, Colombo.
Fleming, R. L. Jr., & R. L. Fleming, Sr. 1973. Some snakes from Nepal. *J. Bombay nat. Hist. Soc.* 70(3):426–437.
Frost, D. R., & D. M. Hillis. 1990. Species in concept and practise: Herpetological applications. *Herpetologica* 46:87–104.
Frost, D. R., A. G. Kluge, & D. M. Hillis. 1992. Species in contemporary herpetology: Comments on phylogenetic inference and taxonomy. *Herpetol. Rev.* 23:46–54.
Gans, C. 1966. Liste der rezenten Amphibien und Reptilien. Uropeltidae. *Tierreich* 84:1–29.
Gans, C. 1992. The status of herpetology. *In*: Herpetology: Current research on the biology of amphibians and reptiles. pp: 7–20. K. Adler (ed). Society for the Study of Amphibians and Reptiles, Contrib. Herpetol. No. 9.
Gadgil, M., & V. M. Meher-Homji. 1990. Ecological diversity. *In*: Conservation in developing countries: Problems and prospects. pp: 175–198. J. C. Daniel & J. S. Serrao (eds). Bombay Natural History Society/Oxford University Press, Bombay.
Gascoyne, M., G. J. Benjamin, & H. P. Schwartz. 1979. Sea-level lowering during the Illinoian glaciation from a Bahama "blue hole". *Science* 205:806–808.
Gaston, A. J. 1990. Forests and forest policy in Northwest India since 1800. *In*: Conservation in developing countries: Problems and prospects. pp: 241–251. J. C. Daniel & J. S. Serrao (eds). Bombay Natural History Society/Oxford University Press, Bombay.
Groombridge, B. 1990. Comments on the rainforests of southwest India and their herpetofauna. *In*: Conservation in developing countries: Problems and prospects. pp: 220–232. J. C. Daniel & J. S. Serrao (eds). Bombay Natural History Society/Oxford University Press, Bombay.
Gruber, U. 1981. Notes on the herpetofauna of Kashmir and Ladakh. *British J. Herpetol.* 6:145–150.

Gupta, R. K. 1986. The Thar Desert. *In*: Ecosystems of the world. Vol. 12B. Hot deserts and arid scrublands. B. pp: 55–99. M. Evenari, I. Noy-Meir & D. W. Goodall (eds). Elsevier, Amsterdam, Oxford, New York and Tokyo.

Gyi, K. K. 1970. A revision of colubrid snakes of the subfamily Homalopsinae. *Univ. Kansas Publ., Mus. nat. Hist.* 20:47–223.

Heaney, L. R. 1986. Biogeography of mammals of SE Asia: estimates of rates of colonization, extinction and speciation. *Biol. J. Linn. Soc.* 28:127–165.

Hoffman, T. W. 1990. Wildlife conservation in Sri Lanka. *In*: Conservation in developing countries: Problems and prospects. pp: 260–266. J. C. Daniel & J. S. Serrao (eds). Bombay Natural History Society/Oxford University Press, Bombay.

Hoge, A. R., & S. A. R. W. L. Romano-Hoge. 1981. Poisonous snakes of the world. Part I. Check list of the pit vipers Viperoidea, Viperidae, Crotalinae. *Mem. Inst. Butantan* 42–43:179–310.

Hora, S. L. 1949. Satpura hypothesis of the distribution of the Malayan fauna and flora to Peninsular India. *Proc. Nat. Inst. Sci. India* 15:207–422.

Huang, Z.-Y. 1982. A new species of the Crotalidae snake from Tibetan. *Acta Fudan Univ. Nat. Sci., Shanghai* 21(3):116–118. [In Chinese with English abstract.]

Inger, R. F. 1960. A revision of the Oriental toads of the genus *Ansonia* Stoliczka. *Fieldiana Zool.* 39:473–503.

Inger, R. F. 1980. Densities of floor-dwelling frogs and lizards in lowland forests in southeast Asia and central America. *Amer. Nat.* 115:761–770.

Inger, R. F., & W. C. Brown. 1980. Species of the scincid genus *Dasia* Gray. *Fieldiana Zool.* 3:1–11.

Inger, R. F., & S. K. Dutta. 1986. An overview of the amphibian fauna of India. *J. Bombay nat. Hist. Soc.* 83:135–146.

Inger, R. F., H. B. Shaffer, M. Koshy, & R. Bakde. 1984. A report on a collection of amphibians and reptiles from the Ponmudi, Kerala, south India. *J. Bombay nat. Hist. Soc.* 81:406–426, 551–570.

Iverson, J. B. 1992a. A revised checklist with distribution maps of the turtles of the world. Privately printed, Richmond, Indiana.

Iverson, J. B. 1992b. Species richness maps of the freshwater and terrestrial turtles of the world. *Smithsonian Herpteol. Inf. Serv.* (88):1–18.

Jaccard, P. 1908. Nouvelles recherches sur la distribution florale. *Bull. Soc. Vaud. Sci. Nat.* 5:223–270.

Jansen, M., & N. De Zoysa. 1992. Sri Lanka's biodiversity: A rapidly diminishing resource. *Tigerpaper* 19:18–24.

Jayaram, K. C. 1974. Ecology and distribution of fresh-water fishes, amphibia and reptiles. *In*: Ecology and biogeography in India. pp: 517–584. M. S. Mani (ed). W. Junk, The Hague.

Khan, M. S. 1985a. An interesting collection of amphibians and reptiles from Cholistan Desert, Pakistan. *J. Bombay nat. Hist. Soc.* 82:144–148.

Khan, M. S. 1985b. Taxonomic notes on *Bungarus caeruleus* (Schneider) and *Bungarus sindanus* Boulenger. *The Snake* 17:71–78.

Kharin, V. E. 1984. A new species of the genus *Hydrophis sensu lato* (Serpentes: Hydrophiidae) from the North Australian Shelf. *Zool. Zh.* 62:1751–1753. [In Russian.]

REFERENCES

King, F. W., & R. L. Burke, 1989. Crocodilian, tuatara, and turtle species of the world: A taxonomic and geographic reference. Association of Systematics Collections, Washington, D. C.

Kluge, A. G. 1991. Checklist of gekkonoid lizards. *Smithsonian Herpetol. Inf. Serv.* (85):1–35.

Kluge, A. G. 1993a. *Calabaria* and the phylogeny of erycine snakes. *Zool. J. Linn. Soc.* 107:293–351.

Kluge, A. G. 1993b. Gekkonoid lizard taxonomy. International Gecko Society, San Diego.

Kottelat, M. 1989. Zoogeography of the fishes from Indochinese inland waters with an annotated checklist. *Bull. Zoöl. Mus., Univ. Amsterdam* 12:1–56.

Krishna Raju, K. S. R., A. V. R. G. Krishna Murthy, C. Subba Reddi, N. A. V. Prasad Reddy, R. Lokaranjan, & K. J. N. G. Shankar 1987. Status of wildlife and habitat conservation in Andhra Pradesh. *J. Bombay nat. Hist. Soc.* 84:605–619.

Krishna Raju, K. S. R., & C. Subba Rao. 1990. Eco-developmental strategies for the Eastern Ghats. *In*: Conservation in developing countries: Problems and prospects. pp: 207–211. J. C. Daniel & J. S. Serrao (eds). Bombay Natural History Society/Oxford University Press, Bombay.

Lack, D. 1976. Island biology illustrated by the land birds of Jamaica. Blackwells, Oxford.

Lawlor, T. E. 1986. Comparative biogeography of mammals on islands. *Biol. J. Linn. Soc.* 28:99–125.

Lazell, J. D., J. E. Keirans, & G. A. Samuelson, 1991. The Sulawesi black racer, *Coluber (Ptyas) dipsas*, and a remarkable parasitic aggregation. *Pacific Sci.* 45:355–361.

Legris, P., & V. M. Meher-Homji. 1982. The Eastern Ghats: vegetation and bioclimatic aspects. *In*: Proc. Nat. Seminar Resource Dev. & Environ. Eastern Ghats. pp: 1–17. Andhra University Press, Waltair.

Lekagul, B., & J. A. McNeely. 1988. Mammals of Thailand. Second edition. Association for the Conservation of Wildlife, Bangkok.

McCann, J. 1945. Reptiles and amphibians of Vizagapatnam and neighbouring Ghats. *J. Bombay nat. Hist. Soc.* 45:435–436.

Mackay, E. J. H. 1934. Further excavations of Mohenjodaro. *J. Roy. Soc. Anthropol.* 10:206.

McKitrick, M. C., & R. M. Zink. 1988. Species concept in ornithology. *Condor* 90:1–14.

Magurran, A. E. 1988. Ecological diversity and its measurement. Croom Helm, London.

Mahendra, B. C. 1939. The zoogeography of India in the light of herpetological studies. *Sci. & Cult.* 4:1–11.

Malnate, E. V. 1960. Systematic division and evolution of the colubrid snake genus *Natrix*, with comments on the subfamily Natricinae. *Proc. Acad. nat. Sci. Philadelphia* 112:41–71.

Malnate, E. V., & G. Underwood, 1988. Australasian natricine snakes of the genus *Tropidonophis*. *Proc. Acad. nat. Sci. Philadelphia* 140:59–201.

Malhotra, A., & K. Davis. 1991. A report on a herpetological survey of the Srivilliputtur Reserve Forest, Tamil Nadu. *J. Bombay nat. Hist. Soc.* 88:157–166.
Mani, M. S. 1974a. Physical features. *In*: Ecology and biogeography in India. pp: 1–50. M. S. Mani (ed). W. Junk, The Hague.
Mani, M. S. 1974b. Biogeography of the peninsula. *In*: Ecology and biogeography in India. pp: 614–647. M. S. Mani (ed). W. Junk, The Hague.
Mani, M. S. 1974c. Biogeography of the eastern borderlands. *In*: Ecology and biogeography in India. pp: 648–681. M. S. Mani (ed). W. Junk, The Hague.
Mani, M. S. 1974d. Biogeography of the western borderlands. *In*: Ecology and biogeography in India. pp: 682–688. M. S. Mani (ed). W. Junk, The Hague.
Mani, M. S. 1974e. Biogeography and evolution in India. *In*: Ecology and biogeography in India. pp: 698–724. M. S. Mani (ed). W. Junk, The Hague.
Mathew, R. 1983. On a collection of snakes from north-east India (Reptilia: Serpentes). *Rec. Zool. Surv. India* 80:449–458.
Mathur, Y. K. 1984. Cenozoic palynofossils, vegetation, ecology and climate of the North and Northwestern Subhimalayan region, India. *In*: The evolution of the east Asian environments. pp: 504–551. R. O. Whyte (ed). Centre for Asian Studies, University of Hong Kong, Hong Kong.
Marx, H. 1988. The colubrid snake, *Psammophis schokari*, from the Arabian peninsula. *Fieldiana Zool. n.s.* (40):1–16.
Mayr, E. 1942. Systematics and the origin of species. Columbia University Press, New York.
Mayr, E. 1963. Animal species and evolution. Harvard University Press, Cambridge, Massachusetts.
Mayr, E. 1976. Evolution and the diversity of life. Harvard University Press, Cambridge, Massachusetts.
Meher-Homji, V. M. 1990. Vegetation types of India in relation to environmental conditions. *In*: Conservation in developing countries: Problems and prospects. pp: 95–110. J. C. Daniel & J. S. Serrao (eds). Bombay Natural History Society/ Oxford University Press, Bombay.
Meher-Homji, V. M., & F. P. Bharucha. 1975. Phytogeography of the Thar region. *In*: Environmental analysis of the Thar Desert. pp: 237–273. R. K. Gupta & I. Prakash (eds). English Book Depot, Dehra Dun.
Mertens, R. 1969. Die amphibiens und reptilien West-Pakistans. *Stutt. Beitr. Naturk.* (197):1–96.
Minton, S. A. 1966. A contribution to the herpetology of West Pakistan. *Bull. American Mus. nat. Hist.* 134:27–184.
Misra, R. 1983. Indian savannas. *In*: Ecosystems of the world. 13. Tropical savannas. pp: 151–166. F. Bourlière (ed). Elsevier Scientific Publishing Company, Amsterdam, Oxford and New York.
Mittleman, M. B. 1952. A generic synopsis of the lizards of the subfamily Lygosominae. *Smithsonian Misc. Coll.* 117:1–35.
Moll, E. O., G. Groombridge, & J. Vijaya. 1986. Redescription of the cane turtle with notes on its natural history and classification. *J. Bombay nat. Hist. Soc.* 83: 112–126.

REFERENCES 83

Molnar, P., & P. Tapponier. 1975. Cenozoic tectonics of Asia: Effects of a continental collision. *Science* 189:419–426.

Monga, S., & B. Sahgal. 1990. The green heart of India. *Sanctuary Asia* 10:16–31, 59–76.

Moody, S. M. 1980. Phylogenetic and historical biogeographical relationships of the genera in the family Agamidae (Reptilia: Lacertilia). Ph.D. Dissertation, University of Michigan.

Morain, S. A. 1984. Systematic and regional biogeography. Van Nostrand Reinhold Company, New York.

Morley, R. J., & J. R. Flenley. 1987. Late Cenozoic vegetational and environmental changes in the Malay Archipelago. *In*: Biogeographic evolution of the Malay Archipelago. pp: 50–59. T. C. Whitmore (ed). Oxford Monographs on Biogeography. Clarendon Press, Oxford.

Mukherjee, A. K. 1966. Extinct and vanishing birds and mammals of India. Indian Museum, Calcutta.

Murthy, T. S. N. 1985. Classification and distribution of the reptiles of India. *The Snake* 17:48–71.

Murthy, T. S. N. 1986. Reptiles of Silent Valley. *Rec. Zool. Surv. India* 84:173–184.

Murthy, T. S. N., & B. D. Sharma. 1976. A contribution to the herpetology of Jammu and Kashmir. *British J. Herpetol.* 5:533–538.

Murthy, T. S. N., B. D. Sharma, & T. Sharma. 1979. Second report on the herpetofauna of Jammu and Kashmir, India. *The Snake* 11:234–241.

Myers, N. 1988. Threatened biotas: "Hotspots" in tropical forests. *The Environmentalist* 8:1–20.

Nanayakkara, G. L. A. 1991. Conservation of the snakes of Sri Lanka. *Hamadryad* 16:46–47.

Nanhoe, L. M. R., & P. E. Ouboter. 1987. The distribution of reptiles and amphibians in the Annapurna-Dhaulagiri regions (Nepal). *Zool. Verh.* (240):1–105.

Numata, M. 1983. Structure and dynamics of vegetation in eastern Nepal. University of Chiba, Chiba.

Obst, F. J. 1983. Zur Kenninis der schlangengattung *Vipera* (Reptilia, Serpentes, Viperidae). *Zool. Abh.* 38:229–235.

Ota, H., & T. Hikida. 1991. Taxonomic review of the lizards of the genus *Calotes* Cuvier 1817 (Agamidae: Squamata) from Sabah, Malaysia. *Trop. Zool.* 4:179–192.

Parenti, L. R. 1990. Sociology and biogeography: a reply to Grehan. *J. Biogeogr.* 17:691.

Pascal, J. P. 1988. Wet evergreen forests of the Western Ghats: Ecology, structure, floristic composition and succession. Institut Français de Pondicherry, Tome 20.

Paterson, D. 1993. Did Tibet cool the world? *New Scientist* 139:29–33.

Pilgrim, G. E. 1937. Fossil antelopes and oxen of the Siwalik hills. *Bull. Amer. Mus. Nat. Hist.* 71:729–874.

Pillai, R. S., & T. S. N. Murthy. 1983. The herpetofauna of the Eastern Ghats. *In*: Proc. Nat. Seminar Resource Dev. & Environ. Eastern Ghats. pp: 81–84. Andhra University Press, Waltair.

Prater, S. H. 1980. The book of Indian animals. Bombay Natural History Society, Bombay.
Preu, C., & W. Erdelen. 1992. Geoecological consequences of human impacts on forests in Sri Lanka. *In*: Tropical forests in transition. pp: 147–164. J. G. Goldammer (ed). Birkhäuser Verlag, Basel.
Ramdas, K. 1992. The forests. *In*: Insight guides: Indian wildlife. pp: 57–62. S. Israel & T. Sinclair (eds). Second edition. APA Publications (HK) Ltd., Singapore.
Randhawa, M. S. 1945. Progressive dessication of northern India. *J. Bombay nat. Hist. Soc.* 45:558–565.
Rao, A. S. 1974. The vegetation and phytogeography of Assam-Burma. *In*: Ecology and biogeography in India. pp: 204–246. M. S. Mani (ed). W. Junk, The Hague.
Rau, M. A. 1974. Vegetation and phytogeography of the Himalayas. *In*: Ecology and biogeography in India. pp: 247–280. M. S. Mani (ed). W. Junk, The Hague.
Reed, T. M. 1987. Island birds and isolation: Lack revisited. *Biol. J. Linn. Soc.* 30:25–29.
Richards, P. W. 1952. The tropical rain forest. Cambridge University Press, Cambridge.
Ripley, S. D., & B. M. Beehler. 1989. Ornithogeographical affinities of the Andaman and Nicobar Islands. *J. Biogeogr.* 16:323–332.
Ripley, S. D., & B. M. Beehler. 1990. Patterns of speciation in Indian birds. *J. Biogeogr.* 17:639–648.
Ripley, S. D., B. M. Beehler, & K. S. R. Krishna Raju, 1987. Birds of the Visakhapatnam Ghats, Andhra Pradesh. *J. Bombay nat. Hist. Soc.* 84:540–559.
Roberts, T. J. 1977. The mammals of Pakistan, Ernest Benn Limited, London and Tonbridge.
Sanyal, D. P., & G. Dasgupta. 1990. On a collection of reptiles from Bastar District, Madhya Pradesh, central India. *Hamadryad* 15:18–20.
Sanyal, D. P., B. Dattagupta, & N. C. Gayen. 1993. Reptilia. *In*: Fauna of Andhra Pradesh. Part I. pp: 1–63. Zoological Survey of India, Calcutta.
Sapru, B. L., & P. Kachroo. 1979. Bio-spectral analysis of Ladakh vegetation. *J. Bombay nat. Hist. Soc.* 74:621–626.
Savage, J. M. 1952. Two centuries of confusion: The history of the snake name *Ahaetulla*. *Bull. Chicago Acad. Sci.* 9:203–216.
Schall, J. J., & E. R. Pianka. 1977. Species densities of reptiles and amphibians on the Iberian Peninsula. *Doñana, Acta Vertebrata* 4:27–34.
Sharma, R. C. 1965. The reptile fauna of the Nagarjunasagar Dam area (Andhra Pradesh, India). *Rec. Zool. Surv. India* 63:77–93.
Simpson, G. G. 1961. Principles of animal taxonomy. Columbia University Press, New York.
Simpson, G. G. 1962. Evolution and geography. Oregon State System of Higher Education, Eugene.
Singh, V. 1978. Phytogeographical reassessment of the flora of Rajasthan. *J. Bombay nat. Hist. Soc.* 74:444–452.
Sinha, A. R. P. 1992. Impacts of growing population and tourism on the endemic flora of Andaman and Nicobar Islands. *Env. Conserv.* 19:173–174, 182.

Smith, A. G., & J. C. Briden. 1977. Mesozoic and Cenozoic Paleocontinental maps. Cambridge University Press, Cambridge.

Smith, H. M. 1989. The original description of *Ovophis* Burger (Serpentes: Viperidae). *Bull. Chicago Herpetol. Soc.* 24:7.

Smith, M. A. 1931. Fauna of British India, including Ceylon and Burma. Vol. I. Loricata, Testudines, Taylor and Francis, London.

Smith, M. A. 1935. Fauna of British India, including Ceylon and Burma. Vol. II. Sauria. Taylor and Francis, London.

Smith, M. A. 1940. The herpetology of the Andaman and Nicobar Islands. *Proc. Linn. Soc.* 1940:150–158.

Smith, M. A. 1943. Fauna of British India, Ceylon and Burma, including the whole of the Indo-Chinese region. Vol. III. Serpentes. Taylor and Francis, London.

Subba Rao, G. V., N. C. Nair, & G. R. Kumari. 1982. Plant resources of the Eastern Ghats. *In*: Proc. Nat. Seminar Resource Dev. & Environ. Eastern Ghats. pp: 27–33. Andhra University Press, Waltair.

Subramanyam, K., & M. P. Nayar. 1974. Vegetation and phytogeography of the Western Ghats. *In*: Ecology and biogeography in India. pp: 178–196. M. S. Mani (ed). W. Junk, The Hague.

Swan, L. W. 1993. The Satpura Hypothesis: A biogeographic challenge to geology. *J. Bombay nat. Hist. Soc.* 90:141–157.

Swan, L. W., & A. E. Leviton. 1962. The herpetofauna of Nepal: A history, check list, and zoogeographic analysis of the herpetofauna. *Proc. Calif. Acad. Sci.* 32:103–147.

Taylor, E. H. 1950. A brief review of Ceylonese snakes. *Univ. Kansas Sci. Bull.* 33:519–603.

Taylor, E. H. 1953. A review of the lizards of Ceylon. *Univ. Kansas Sci. Bull.* 35:1525–1585.

Tikader, B. K., & R. C. Sharma. 1992. Handbook: Indian lizards. Zoological Survey of India, Calcutta.

Van der Hammen, T. 1983. The palaeoecology and palaeogeography of savannas. *In*: Ecosystems of the world. 13. Tropical savannas. pp: 19–35. F. Bourlière (ed). Elsevier Scientific Publishing Company, Amsterdam, Oxford and New York.

Vitt, L. J. 1987. Communities. *In*: Snakes: Ecology and evolutionary biology. pp: 335–365. R. A. Seigel, J. T. Collins & S. S. Novak (eds). McGraw-Hill Publishing Company, New York.

Waltner, R. C. 1975a. Geographical and altitudinal distribution of amphibians and reptiles in the Himalayas. Part I. *Cheetal* 16:17–25.

Waltner, R. C. 1975b. Geographical and altitudinal distribution of amphibians and reptiles in the Himalayas. Part II. *Cheetal* 16:28–36.

Waltner, R. C. 1975c. Geographical and altitudinal distribution of amphibians and reptiles in the Himalayas. Part III. *Cheetal* 16:14–19.

Waltner, R. C. 1975d. Geographical and altitudinal distribution of amphibians and reptiles in the Himalayas. Part IV. *Cheetal* 16:12–17.

Webb, R. G. 1995. Redescription and neotype designation of *Pelochelys bibroni* from Southern New Guinea (Testudines: Trionychidae). *Chel. Conserv. & Biol.* 1:301–310.

Welch, K. R. G. 1988. Snakes of the Orient: A checklist. Robert E. Krieger Publishing Company, Malabar, Florida.
Welch, K. R. G., P. S. Cooke, & A. S. Wright. 1990. Lizards of the Orient: A checklist. Robert E. Krieger Publishing Company, Malabar, Florida.
Whitaker, R. 1978. Herpetological survey in the Andamans. *Hamadryad* 3:9–16.
Whitaker, R. 1985. Managing tropical forests: Endangered Andamans. Environmental Services Group, World Wildlife Fund - India & MAB India, Department of Environment, New Delhi.
White, G. B. 1981. Semispecies, sibling species and superspecies. *In*: The evolving biosphere: Chance, change and challenge. pp: 21–28. P. L. Forey (ed). British Museum (Natural History)/Cambridge University Press, London.
Whitmore, T. C. 1987. Introduction. *In*: Biogeographical evolution of the Malay Archipelago. pp: 1–4. T. C. Whitmore (ed). Clarendon Press, Oxford.
Wilkinson, L. 1990. SYSTAT: The system for statistics. SYSTAT, Inc., Evanston, Illinois.
Wüster, W., S. Otsuka, A. Malhotra, & R. S. Thorpe. 1992. Population systematics of Russell's viper: A multivariate study. *Biol. J. Linn. Soc.* 47:97–113.
Wüster, W., & R. S. Thorpe. 1989. Population affinities of the Asiatic cobra (*Naja naja*) species complex in southeast Asia: Reliability and random resampling. *Biol. J. Linn. Soc.* 36:391–409.
Yasukawa, Y., H. Ota, & T. Hikida. 1992. Taxonomic re-evaluation of the two subspecies of *Geoemyda spengleri* (Gmelin, 1789) (Reptilia): Emydidae). *Japanese J. Herpetol.* 14:143–159.

INDEX

Afro-Mediterranean elements, 21, 22, 23, 24, 26, 29, 68, 75
archipelago effect, 31
area cladogram, 26
barrier, 21, 34
Biological Species Concept, 4
center of origin, 19, 25
cluster analysis, 3, 26
Coefficient of Community, 3, 25, 29
disjunct distribution, 28, 30, 35
dispersal, 28, 32, 33, 34, 73, 76
endemicity, 13, 17, 18, 21, 22, 23, 24, 27, 64, 65
Evolutionary Species Concept, 4, 17, 23, 35
extralimital elements, 28
faunal speciation, 31
Filippino elements, 23, 70
filter (biological), 29, 32
Indian radiation, 22, 23, 70, 75
Indo-Malayan elements, 21, 22, 23, 24, 25, 29, 30, 69, 75
intergradient population, 32
Jaccard's Index, 3
niche, 19, 25, 75
oceanic elements, 70
Oriental elements, 1, 20, 24, 29, 72, 75
over-water dispersal, 21
Palaearctic elements, 1, 20, 23, 24, 26, 28, 29, 72
parapatric model, 34
refugial model, 33, 34, 73, 76
relict species, 32
Satpura Hypothesis, 28
sister species, 31, 33, 73, 76
species diversity, 17, 18, 21, 24, 25, 75
species richness, 17

Tibeto-Yunnanese elements, 21, 22, 24, 29, 69
transitional genera, 19, 23, 71, 72
Turkomanian–Central Asian elements, 21, 23, 24, 29, 68, 75
unknown elements, 71
vicariance, 33, 34, 73, 76